The Art of Dying

american
university
studies

Series XXIV
American Literature

Vol. 56

PETER LANG
New York • Washington, D.C./Baltimore • Bern
Frankfurt am Main • Berlin • Brussels • Vienna • Oxford

Deborah S. Gentry

The Art of Dying

Suicide in the Works
of Kate Chopin and Sylvia Plath

PETER LANG
New York • Washington, D.C./Baltimore • Bern
Frankfurt am Main • Berlin • Brussels • Vienna • Oxford

Library of Congress Cataloging-in-Publication Data

Gentry, Deborah S. (Deborah Suiter).
The art of dying: suicide in the works of Kate Chopin
and Sylvia Plath / Deborah S. Gentry.
p. cm. — (American University studies; XXIV.
American literature; v. 56.)
Includes bibliographical references.
1. Chopin, Kate, 1851–1904. Awakening. 2. Plath, Sylvia. Bell jar.
3. Suicide in literature. 4. Women in literature. 5. Sex role in literature.
6. Women—Psychology. 7. Women—Identity. 8. Women—Sexual
behavior. 9. Women—Social conditions. I. Title.
PS1294.C63G46   810.9'3548—dc22   2006025137
ISBN 978-0-8204-2496-5
ISSN 0895-0512

Bibliographic information published by **Die Deutsche Bibliothek**.
Die Deutsche Bibliothek lists this publication in the "Deutsche
Nationalbibliografie"; detailed bibliographic data is available
on the Internet at http://dnb.ddb.de/.

The paper in this book meets the guidelines for permanence and durability
of the Committee on Production Guidelines for Book Longevity
of the Council of Library Resources.

Printed in Germany

TABLE OF CONTENTS

ACKNOWLEDGMENTS

THE COLOSSUS AND OTHER POEMS by Sylvia Plath. Copyright @ 1962 by Sylvia Plath. Used with permission of Alfred A. Knopf, a division of Random House, Inc.

THE COLLECTED POEMS by Sylvia Plath, edited by Ted Hughes. Copyright @ 1981 by Sylvia Plath. Reprinted with permission of Faber and Faber.

THE BELL JAR by Sylvia Plath. Copyright @ 1963 by Sylvia Plath. Reprinted with the permission of Faber and Faber and HarperCollins.

CHAPTER I

Introduction:
The Paradigm of Women's Suicide

In his best known theoretical work of literary criticism, "The Philosophy of Composition," Edgar Allan Poe states his theory of what constitutes good poetry: the proper subject of poetry is beauty and the most legitimate tone is melancholy. To produce this effect, according to Poe, the best subject for poetry is death allied with beauty. Thus, he concludes that "the death, then, of a beautiful woman is, unquestionably, the most poetical topic in the world" (158). Poe describes here one of the most common of literary symbols, the untimely death of a beautiful woman, and states overtly a major preoccupation of Romantic art. However resonant this symbolic death might be in Western literature, that symbolism has been principally developed in the hands of men for primarily masculine appreciation. A crucial question thus becomes: what does the death of a beautiful woman mean to women who have become artists in a trade dominated by masculine motifs? Whereas it is clear that projections of death onto women characters allow male writers to distance and objectify the experience of death, what does that same death mean in works written by women about women, especially when that death is due to suicide? The purpose of this book is to answer that question at least in part by studying the works of some representative women writers, particularly Kate Chopin and Sylvia Plath, to determine what role suicide plays in their work.

From the very beginnings of Western literature, from Greek tragedy, women's suicides have been portrayed as central plot elements. Jocasta, a major character, kills herself in *Oedipus Rex*, and more significantly, Antigone, the protagonist, martyrs herself heroically in *Antigone*. Margaret Higonnet notes in her brilliant essay "Speaking Silences: Women's Suicide":

> Classical instances of women's suicide are perceived as masculine: Antigone, Cleopatra, Hasdrubal's wife, and Arria, who stabbed herself to encourage her husband and said, *Paete, non dolet*. Charlotte Corday, the self-appointed Girondiste martyr of the French Revolution, is one of the last of this tradition. (70)

The "masculine" tradition that Higonnet refers to is one where the act of suicide is seen as a choice made of the victim's free will and intended as a symbolic act of defiance or protest against tyranny or immorality. This kind of suicide in literature is intended to move the surviving characters to embrace strong action to remedy a perceived social or political problem.

However, as Higonnet points out, with the advent of the Age of Reason in the eighteenth century, suicide increasingly becomes identified with weakness and mental instability. Under this view, suicide is no longer conceived of as an heroic act of free will but an involuntary act of a weak mind. Higonnet states that "the very notion of suicide as an intentional act dissipates in the course of its scientific reassessment" to the point that by the nineteenth century, suicide has been completely "feminized" into a passive act (70). Of this transition, Higonnet writes:

> In the Romantic period, the focus of aesthetics shifts from action (Aristotle) to character (Herder, Coleridge). Accordingly, in literary depictions of suicide, the focus shifts from function to motive. At the same time, the stock motives for suicide narrow in range and become more "feminine" than in classical times. After the French Revolution, voluntary death is depoliticized. This pattern is visible in the case of men as well as women. (71)

Higonnet uses examples from the poetry of Keats, Shelley, and Wagner to underscore the new identification by the Man of Sensibility with the Dionysian experience of romantic love.

Despite some prominent examples of male suicides in literature, Higonnet concludes that in the nineteenth-century, the literary motif of suicide features primarily women victims, although in reality women commit suicide at a much lower rate than men. She states:

> This nineteenth-century reorientation of suicide toward love, passive self-surrender, and illness seems particularly evident in the literary depiction of women; their self-destruction is most often perceived as motivated by love, understood not only as loss of self but as surrender to an illness: *le mal d'amour*. (71)

The point that Higonnet is making is consistent with one of the main themes of Sandra Gilbert and Susan Gubar's monumental work *The Madwoman in the Attic: The Woman Writer and the Nineteenth-Century*

Literary Imagination. In this work, Gilbert and Gubar extensively explore the recurring themes in women's literature that arise from women's peculiar position in a patriarchical society. According to them, women have internalized the notion that they "exist only to be acted on by men, both as literary and as sensual objects" (8). Rather than create art, women are themselves supposed to be works of art. In order to be works of art, women must subordinate their individuality, or according to Gilbert and Gubar, kill themselves "into a 'perfect' image" (14). This perfect image is Coventry Patmore's "angel in the house." As Gilbert and Gubar point out,

> Whether she becomes an *objet d'art* or a saint, however, it is the surrender of self—of her personal comfort, her personal desires, or both—that is the beautiful angel-woman's key act, while it is precisely this sacrifice, which dooms her both to death and heaven. For to be selfless is not only to be noble, it is to be dead. A life that has no story…is really a life of death, a death-in-life. (25)

The numerous pale and consumptive heroines who appear in Victorian and Edwardian literature are representations of the angel, as are the children who die young in works like *Little Women* and *Uncle Tom's Cabin.*

The alternative option portrayed for women is to become the monster, the madwoman in the attic of *Jane Eyre* or the fallen woman, or simply the woman who selfishly puts her interests before those of others. In an analysis of folk tales, Gilbert and Gubar observe that if the angel is Snow White, the monster is her wicked step-mother. The rapacious monster is associated with a woman's sexuality, with madness, and with the most repellent and unnatural of acts, even the killing of her children.

Of course, the portrayal of women as either angels or monsters in literature and in culture in general has led to much anguish for women in real life. Typically, the internalization of these conflicting images has become paralyzing to the psychological development of many women, as is amply portrayed in Sylvia Plath's *The Bell Jar*, where the protagonist Esther Greenwood feels she must be one or the other rather than an integration of the two that constitutes psychological maturity. However, if Esther feels that she has a choice, most women do not, because the monster has been presented as evil incarnate. Gilbert and Gubar state:

> The sexual nausea associated with all these monster women helps explain why so many real women have for so long expressed loathing of (or at least anxiety about)

their own, inexorably female bodies. The "killing" of oneself into an art object—
the pruning and preening, the mirror madness, and concern with odors and aging,
with hair which is invariably too curly or too lank, with bodies too thin or too
thick—all this testifies to the efforts women have expended not just trying to be
angels but trying *not* to become female monsters. (34)

No wonder Gilbert and Gubar conclude that the story of the female
protagonist in literature often seems to end in her doom: "The cycle of her fate
seems inexorable. Renouncing 'contemplative purity,' she must now embark
on the life of 'significant action' which, for a woman, is defined as a witch's
life because it is so monstrous, so unnatural" (42). In life and in literature,
women live balanced between these two extremes in a purgatory of guilt and
self-doubt. Gilbert and Gubar lament for the typical female heroine in
literature: "Her only deed...can be the deed of death, her only action, the
pernicious action of self-destruction" (42). This twilight world in which the
heroine seeks a life of significant action within the constraints of a
patriarchical society concerns Chopin and Plath, and it is not surprising that
their heroines choose suicide as a way out of this trap.

As Gilbert and Gubar have demonstrated, since a woman's identity more
so than a man's is bound up in her physical body, woman as artist often uses
the female body as a means of expressing herself. In literature, as well as in
life, a woman's chastity or purity becomes the battlefield for the sexual
politics of men and women. In support of this idea, Higonnet draws an
interesting connection between women as sexual beings and as capitalistic
commodities. She notes that women who become damaged goods, as it were,
due to their loss of purity are degraded as a commodity by patriarchical
society, in other words, in terms of their marriageability. In literature, women
who no longer wish to be dominated by men and be considered a commodity
sometimes express their rebellion through sexual promiscuity, and female
promiscuity is in turn defined as a sign of mental illness by a masculine
society. This is another instance of society's tendency to label as insane any
behavior that it does not condone, denying those who are different a legitimate
voice to be heard. Beth Bassein points out the consequences of female
promiscuity in literature:

Death plays a major role in all literature, but women and men are depicted quite
differently when they are subjected to death-producing experiences or to death

itself…[O]ne of the chief differences is that the sexual side of the woman is far
more often responsible for her death than it is for the male. (80)

Clearly, the message is being sent that sexual freedom for women can result in
physical or psychological death, or both.

Perhaps the two most prominent examples of female protagonists who
attempt to experience sexual freedom in nineteenth-century literature are Anna
Karenina and Emma Bovary, both of whom are characters invented by male
writers. It is illuminating to compare and contrast these two suicides with the
suicides of female characters written by female writers, especially in light of
the theories established by Higonnet and Gilbert and Gubar.

In Leo Tolstoy's *Anna Karenina*, Anna demonstrates the two
precipitating factors for female suicide in literature that Higonnet has
outlined—*mal d'amour* and sexual freedom. By abandoning her husband and
son for the illicit love of Count Vronsky, she becomes caught in the flux of
social forces beyond her control. She is seen as a fallen woman by society, a
social outlaw. Her dilemma produces depression and ambivalence, with Anna
first embracing one action then another as a possible solution to her plight, but
as Katherine Henley concludes of Anna in "Death as Option," "the heroine
has reached an emotional or psychological impasse: she cannot any longer
affect her life positively" (200). Anna's growing confusion is one of the most
striking themes in the scene in the railway station immediately preceding her
death. Constantly, she asks herself why she is here and what she means to do.
In her confusion, Anna becomes overwhelmed with the complications of her
life; Tolstoy presents her as thinking, "Everything that had seemed to her
possible before was now so difficult to consider" (797). Finally, she embraces
suicide as a means out of her situation, but more importantly as a means of
revenge against Vronsky, who she feels has seduced her and then cast her off
for a new conquest. Anna, deciding to throw herself under the train,
triumphantly thinks, "I shall punish him and escape from everyone and from
myself" (798). Henley states, "Her desire to 'punish' Vronsky is a part of her
need to justify her actions" (201).

In her analysis of *Anna Karenina*, Higonnet is distressed by Tolstoy's
portrayal of Anna in this, her last crucial scene:

The feminization of suicide in the nineteenth-century goes hand in hand with a—
realistic yet disturbing—denial of woman's ability to choose freely. Even Anna

Karenina, one of the most compassionately drawn heroines of nineteenth-century fiction, is shown to vacillate in her last moments. Tolstoy makes her act manipulative and vengeful...He also deprives it [Anna's suicide] of dignity through small but acute details. (78)

As Higonnet observes, Anna's ambivalence at the moment of death is the major way in which Tolstoy undercuts her as an agent of free will. Tolstoy words her actual suicide as follows:

And exactly at the moment when the midpoint between the wheels drew level with her, she threw away the red bag, and drawing her head back into her shoulders, fell on her hands under the car, and, with a light movement, as though she would rise immediately, dropped on her knees. And at the instant she was terror-stricken at what she was doing. "Where am I? What am I doing? What for?" She tried to get up to throw herself back; but something huge and merciless struck her on the head and dragged her down on her back. "Lord, forgive me everything!" she said, feeling it impossible to struggle. (798–99)

Anna is more confused and disoriented than she is determined and resolute, and confusion and disorientation are hallmarks of a "feminine" suicide.

It is her inability to struggle against hostile social forces—particularly the image of the monster that her culture associates with sexual freedom in women—that marks Anna's weakness of identity. This weakness, according to Higonnet, disposes one towards suicide: "The breakdown of one's sense of identity is conventionally considered a major factor in suicide by modern psychologists like Horney or Farberow" (72). Higonnet goes on to state:

Where literature links suicide to the disintegration of identity, the catalysts differ by gender. Men identify themselves with their political standing, their heroic self-image...For our fictions of women, suicidal disintegration far more often has to do with their sexual and amorous relationships. Traditionally, myths of female suicide have focused on two themes: defeated love and chastity. (73)

Women's identities are portrayed as bound up inextricably with masculine perceptions of them.

A woman's death as a result of adultery also brings to mind the other famous literary suicide of nineteenth-century literature, Emma Bovary. Gustave Flaubert is generally considered to be a realist, but in *Madame Bovary*, he is satirizing in Emma the illusions of a provincial woman who has read too many romance novels. Margaret Tillett in "On Reading *Madame Bovary*" states:

> Unfortunately Romanticism is all too often represented in life by such as poor Emma Bovary, shoddily pursuing a shoddy ideal, a piece of imitation jewellery [sic] if ever there was one. This bastard Romanticism is what Flaubert is satirizing in *Madame Bovary*. (3)

Beth Bassein echoes Gilbert and Gubar when she concludes that "Emma is one of scores of heroines whose adultery made her into a kind of monster to spook generations of women and critically damage their concept of self" (70). Given the general paradigm of nineteenth-century portrayals of fallen women, Emma's death is foreshadowed by her sexual promiscuity and her overwhelming materialism, symbolized by her financial extravagance.

It is the latter that directly precipitates her suicide. Only when she can no longer buy herself out of a depression does Emma finally embrace the death that has courted her throughout the novel. As her fate closes in on her, she too acts confused, racing around town trying to raise money; but her actions, like Anna Karenina's, are to cross purposes. One moment she is begging various men for money, half believing that she truly loves them, the next she runs to the pharmacy and takes poison. Although Emma would like to think of herself as heroic in her suicide, Flaubert describes her in this final action as being without dignity, like a child at a candy store; she "plunged in her hand, withdrew it full of white powder, and ate greedily" (357). She eats arsenic which, ironically, the pharmacist later tells the authorities she has mistaken for sugar.

Even in the throes of a horrible death, Emma is portrayed as narcissistic, asking for her mirror. Flaubert writes, ". . . she remained bowed over it for some time, until great tears flowed from her eyes" (369). The mirror is not only a symbol of her vanity but also of her femininity. Here Emma parallels Tennyson's Lady of Shallot who can only experience life vicariously through her mirror. As Gilbert and Gubar note, mirrors are important symbols because they show only half of a woman—the false and superficial exterior—without reflecting the self that is contained inside. Mirrors, like glass in general, are associated with women because women experience barriers in life invisible to men and are expected to experience life itself primarily through others. Bassein finds the mirror image extended in Emma's death scene:

> Just as her death rattle becomes stronger, the blind man's song reaches her ears
> from the street and she begins "an atrocious, frantic, desperate laugh," thinking she
> sees the hideous face of the wretch looking out of the darkness and menacing her.
> The old fellow has become her mirror. (79)

In the end, the reader cannot identify with Emma in her ordeal. Under the glare of Flaubert's unrelenting presentation, the excruciating details of her death reduce her in the reader's eyes to the state of a gasping, tortured animal.

Thus we have seen the fates of Anna Karenina and Madame Bovary—woman characters portrayed by male authors. One might assume that a female protagonist would be portrayed quite differently from the perspective of a woman writer, but such a blanket assumption is not true. In fact, most of the commercially successful women writers of the nineteenth century presented viewpoints strikingly similar to those of the men. Although Gilbert and Gubar in *The Madwoman in the Attic* conclude that Jane Eyre and Bertha, Rochester's mad wife, are dual figures—the angel and the monster—or even two sides of the same figure in *Jane Eyre*, in the final analysis, Charlotte Bronte's sympathies are with the couple Rochester and Jane, in opposition to his mad wife. Rochester's attempted bigamy and his manipulation of all the women in the novel are not judged, and the female protagonist's marriage to him in the end is seen as a triumph.

An analysis of Edith Wharton's *The House of Mirth* also shows many similarities to this standard masculine point-of-view. *The House of Mirth* was published in 1905, a year after Kate Chopin's death and five years after *The Awakening* had been published. As Gilbert and Gubar observe in their analysis of Wharton's work in *No Man's Land: The Place of Woman Writer in the Twentieth Century*, she, like Chopin, did not embrace the contemporary women's movement:

> Wharton was emphatically not a feminist in the ordinary sense of the word. On the
> contrary, she seems often to have gone out of her way to present herself as an old-
> fashioned 'man's woman' who felt nothing but contempt for New Womanly
> strivings. (126)

However, just because Wharton was not a suffragette does not mean that she approved of the patriarchical society she wrote about. Wharton was primarily a satirist, and the brunt of her attack was leveled against the old New York high society of which she was a part.

As often happens with victims, Wharton identified more with the oppressor than with the oppressed, an attitude not dissimilar to that of Sylvia Plath. When Plath sought an external metaphor for her internal suffering that was rooted primarily in her sex role anxiety, she often depicted herself as a victim of the Holocaust, associating her sufferings as a woman with that of the Jews of World War II, although she was not herself Jewish and had no direct connection with that experience. With both Wharton and Plath, one feels that the mere plight of women is not quite important enough in itself to constitute the subject matter of tragedy, yet their rage at being born a woman with the consequence of dealing constantly with arbitrary societal limitations translates into the intensity of voice that is a hallmark of their best writings.

Gilbert and Gubar in *No Man's Land* see Wharton's work as a positive contribution to the development of women in literature, concluding that

> despite all this evidence that Edith Wharton was neither in theory nor in practice a feminist, her major fictions, taken together, constitute perhaps the most searching—and searing—feminist analysis of the construction of "femininity" produced by any novelist in this century. (128)

This statement places Wharton at or near the top of Gilbert and Gubar's list of important women writers. Despite this praise, I find, in analyzing one of her most successful novels, *The House of Mirth*, that Wharton's anger does not translate into a better role model for women because ultimately Wharton does not identify with the women characters she creates any more than Flaubert does.

In *The House of Mirth*, Wharton uses the plight of the protagonist Lily Bart to articulate her anger over the artificiality and social determinism of women's lives. Lily, of course, is a commodity, her marriageability her ticket to the life of conspicuous consumption that Thorstein Veblen describes in *The Theory of the Leisure Class* (1899). In that work, Veblen overtly states an understood societal fact that the traditional role of woman has been to serve as an outward and observable symbol of her husband's material success. She renders this service by conspicuously consuming goods that she has not produced and by maintaining a high degree of enforced leisure; in other words, she shops till she drops. As Veblen states:

The leisure rendered by the wife...is, of course, not a simple manifestation of idleness or indolence. It almost invariably occurs disguised under some form of work or household duties or social amenities, which prove on analysis to serve little or no ulterior end beyond showing that she does not and need not occupy herself with anything that is gainful or that is of substantial use

...Not that the results of her attention to household matters, of a decorative and mundificatory character, are not pleasing to the sense of men trained in middle-class proprieties; but the taste to which these effects of household adornment and tidiness appeal is a taste which has been formed under the selective guidance of a canon of propriety that demands just these evidences of wasted effort. (139)

Ultimately, Veblen maintains that the wife is merely a slave, stating, "for the habitual rendering of vicarious leisure and consumption is the abiding mark of the unfree servant" (140). Veblen's theories come to life in Wharton's writings; as Gilbert and Gubar observe, "most of her fiction is focused with cold fury on the limits and liabilities of 'the feminine' in a culture that fashions women to be ornamental, exploitative, and inarticulate" (*No Man's Land* 129).

Poor Lily Bart seems to be the object of Wharton's fury as she mismanages even the small social role that she is assigned, to be ornamental. Wai-Chee Dimock, in "Debasing Exchange: Edith Wharton's *The House of Mirth*," concludes that Lily Bart is ambivalent about her role as a commodity:

Of all the characters, Lily Bart has the most puzzling and contradictory relation to the marketplace. A self-acknowledged "human merchandise," she is busy marketing herself throughout most of the book, worried only about the price she would fetch...And yet her repeated and sometimes intentional failure to find a buyer, her ultimate refusal to realize her "asset"—as her mother designates her beauty—makes her something of a rebel. (783)

However, Lily Bart is a thoroughly socialized female, incapable of a significant or effective rebellion; she is closer to Emma Bovary than Edna Pontellier. And this is precisely the conclusion drawn by Dimock:

She [Lily] is not much of a rebel, of course, and that is precisely the point. For Lily's "rebellion," in its very feebleness and limitation, attests to the frightening power of the marketplace. It attests as well to Wharton's own politics, to her bleakness of vision in the face of a totalizing system she finds at once detestable and inevitable. (783)

As Dimock suggests, Wharton's pessimism led her to depict women as inevitable victims of an exploitative society, a viewpoint which Gilbert and Gubar also underscore. Gilbert and Gubar observe that some critics accuse Wharton of being cold, aloof, and unsympathetic to the plight of her women characters. They attempt to refute this observation by stating that this is the critics' "misperception of the grim delight with which she forced herself, and her readers, to face the social facts that made her women (and their men) what they were" (*No Man's Land* 131). But even Gilbert and Gubar conclude that Wharton pursues her women protagonists' fates with "what feels at times like sickening ferocity" (131). In the case of *The House of Mirth* in particular, Louis Auchincloss says:

> What explains the continuing fascination of this novel is not the moral struggle but the drama of the hunt of a desperate creature by a pack of remorseless hounds. The creature may double back in her tracks, she may bound over streams, and occasionally her pursuers may lose the scent, but so does she lose strength and speed, and the end is inevitable. She never has a chance. She is too beautiful. Lily's beauty is the light in which each of her different groups would like to shine, but when they find that it illuminates their ugliness they want to put it out. (72)

Wharton's unrelenting negative tone is similar to that of Flaubert, who might have contended that "Madame Bovary, *c'est moi*," but who remains clearly aloof from her degradation and destruction in the novel. Lily Bart is also ruined by the same forces that Madame Bovary faces—materialism and romanticism. Thus, we see that in *The House of Mirth*, Wharton's only novel to portray a female protagonist's suicide, her theme and tone are not essentially different from those of prominent male writers who preceded and succeeded her.

As Wharton characterizes her, Lily is also reminiscent of the author F. Scott Fitzgerald and his literary alter-ego, Jay Gatsby. Like Fitzgerald and Gatsby, Lily does not have the financial resources to run in the crowd that she aspires to, and because she is somehow fundamentally different from them in her outlook, she is always slightly separated from that crowd even when among them. Gatsby and Lily are more talked about than talked to, marking them as figures of isolation and loneliness. Also like Gatsby, Lily is ultimately a victim of her innocent romantic illusions, the most intense object of which is Lawrence Selden, a dilettante who shares with Lily the tastes of the upper class but not the means.

Selden, like Robert LeBrun in *The Awakening*, prefers to look but not touch. Faced with the possibility of actually obtaining Lily, Selden flees from her to the Caribbean as Robert flees from Edna to Mexico. Both men prefer the narcissistic control that their illusions give them over the reality of love that would require them to share control of their lives with the beloved. Dimock maintains that Selden is always the spectator of life, judging the actions of those around him. His overriding need is to be in control of his emotions, which is evident in his last conversation with Lily. Selden holds himself aloof from Lily's emotional confessions, but Lily is no longer interested in remaining an observer of life, no matter how superficially beautiful that life is in the world of the upper class. Wharton writes that Lily "had passed beyond the phase of well-bred reciprocity, in which every demonstration must be scrupulously proportioned to the emotion it elicits, and generosity of feeling is the only ostentation condemned" (496). Lily does not want to continue to guard against life and freedom of expression, but to open her doors to experience.

In passing beyond the bounds of polite society in this one way more than any other, Lily now has no option left but suicide. Lily's death is portrayed as saving her from the degradations of daily existence, and as Louis Auchincloss concludes, "we finish the book with the conviction that in the whole brawling, terrible city Lily is the one and only lady" (71). Ironically, it is Auchincloss's apt use of the word "lady" that clearly signifies Wharton's failure to move beyond male stereotypes in her portrayal of Lily. Lily is indeed a "lady," yet another portrayal which resorts to the angel/monster dichotomy that Gilbert and Gubar insist the female artist must move beyond to finally create real, integrated women characters.

If Wharton moves to the brink of a new paradigm for women characters in literature, she distinctly compromises this effort in the novel's conclusion. In fact, Wharton changes diction and tone in the last few pages of the novel when she describes Lily's death and Selden's reaction to it, veering into a tear-jerking ending that was probably very pleasing to her audience. Two of the striking characteristics of Lily Bart throughout the novel are her personal honesty and her grace under pressure. However, as Lily succumbs to the effects of the sleeping medicine she has taken, Wharton sentimentalizes Lily in death; Lily believes that she is nestling the baby of the working class angel,

Nellie Struther. Wharton portrays Lily's last thoughts as follows: "for a moment she seemed to have lost her hold of the child. But no—she was mistaken—the tender pressure of its body was still close to hers: the recovered warmth flowed through her once more, she yielded to it, sank into it, and slept" (523). Of course, this is the baby that Lily and Selden will never have, and what might have been a heroic suicide protesting social limitations on women becomes a sentimental set piece.

Selden, who has always been ready to believe the worst of Lily without bothering to seek explanations from her, seems to change abruptly with her death. In fact, the novel concludes with these two paragraphs, encapsulating Selden's bedside grief at what he had lost:

> It was this moment of love, this fleeting victory over themselves, which had kept them from atrophy and extinction; which, in her, had reached out to him in every struggle against the influence of her surroundings, and in him, had kept alive the faith that now drew him penitent and reconciled to her side.
> He knelt by the bed and bent over her, draining their last moment to its lees; and in the silence there passed between them the word which made all clear. (532)

The major problem with this ending is that Wharton has not prepared the reader for the sentimentalization of Lily Bart in her death scene. But equally shocking is the transformation of Selden into a man far more sensitive to Lily in death than he ever was in life. Although Wharton means for us to read this transformation positively, it is ironically in character for Selden to love Lily more dead than alive. Ultimately, Lily chooses death as the only means to preserve her social status, and, if, as Dimock asserts, *The House of Mirth* is about life as a series of transactions with the price being figured in money and emotion, then in this case Lily is made to pay a high price to be a "lady."

It is important to note that *Anna Karenina*, *Madame Bovary*, and even *The House of Mirth* do not end with the death of the protagonist but continue with the lives of the surrounding characters. In fact, *Madame Bovary* ends only with the death of her husband, Charles. The effect this produces is that the woman's death is important only in how it affects other characters, mostly men, who remain alive, an effect which is striking in the conclusion of Tennyson's poem "The Lady of Shallot." Tennyson is the great mid-Victorian writer about suicide, having written a score of his major poems on the subject. The Lady of Shallot dies for love of the knight Lancelot, ironically without his ever knowing it. The poem concludes not with her death but with Lancelot viewing her corpse and stating, "She has a pretty face," another instance of woman as symbol rather than substance. In his presentation of female suicide as evinced in "The Lady of Shallot," Tennyson portrays Poe's death of a beautiful woman in the Romantic tradition of sacrificing all for love.

In examining three major novels of women's suicides, we have seen that, as Higonnet states, love and chastity become the two double-binds for women in taking control of their lives. If they wish to assert control over their bodies and sexuality, they are considered promiscuous and mentally unstable. If they kill themselves, their deaths are attributed to mental illness or to love. Both characterizations degrade and depersonalize the woman involved.

Much attention has been given thus far to the theories of Higonnet and Gilbert and Gubar because their work delineates the philosophical approach of this book. Now that the literary and historic context has been explored, the contribution that Kate Chopin and Sylvia Plath make can be better analyzed. In contrast to the women protagonists' suicides in *Anna Karenina, Madame Bovary,* and *The House of Mirth,* the subtle but radical departure that Chopin takes in portraying Edna Pontellier's suicide in *The Awakening* becomes more apparent. For the first-time reader, *The Awakening* may appear to be a failure, especially if it is analyzed using the standard literary paradigm of a woman defeated by love. And, in fact, *The Awakening* is often analyzed using that paradigm, even to the extent of labeling the novel as the American *Madame Bovary.* Kenneth Eble makes that connection in his seminal essay that revived interest in Chopin's work. However, he refutes the comparison, concluding that "despite the similarities and possible influences, the novel [*The Awakening*], chiefly because of the independent character of its heroine, Edna Pontellier, and because of the intensity of the focus upon her, is not simply a good but derivative work. It has a manner and matter of its own" (9). As Eble implies, Edna Pontellier's independence makes the novel unique, and it must be read using a different paradigm, a point that will be more fully developed in the next chapter.

In comparing *The Awakening* to *The House of Mirth,* Gilbert and Gubar seem to prefer the latter, concluding that Chopin's Edna "fled into realms of fantasy" while Wharton continues an "unflinching and unremitting exploration" of "the process by which women are socialized as prisoners of sex" (*No Man's Land* 129). Gilbert and Gubar acknowledge that Chopin's

Edna was struggling "to find ways out of the Hisland that so degraded and diminished women" (129), but they see these efforts as ultimately weak attempts to flee from reality. Wharton they characterize as being somehow more heroic because she had a darker vision:

> Wharton mostly saw signs that said NO EXIT. An intransigent realist and a self-defined "priestess of reason," she frankly declared that "life is the saddest thing there is, next to death" and never openly elaborated full-scale fantasies about the liberation and gratification of female desire or about the unleashing of the female power in the ways that more optimistic feminists did. (129)

Of course, this preference is merely personal on Gilbert and Gubar's part; Chopin's Edna Pontellier can just as easily be seen as a heroine on the edge of the existential abyss, the woman who sees Wharton's process of socialization and refuses to be an object anymore. In that light, Wharton's vaunted realism appears a bit more like rationalizing, compromise, and capitulation to the way things are; and one wonders finally which writer speaks to the woman of the twentieth century.

Once Edna's suicide is seen as an heroic act, then several of the more troubling aspects of *The Awakening* fall into place. Many critics are confused by the ending, since they are used to reading female suicide in literature through the paradigm of the feminine suicide, dying for love. Superficially, Edna's death is often interpreted in that light since Edna commits suicide after her final rejection by Robert. However, a careful reading of the novel quickly refutes that point of view as Chapter II will demonstrate. The essential physicality of Edna, the constant descriptions of her physical, animal acts— sleeping, moving, eating—are meant to project more than just her fundamental sexuality. Chopin is clearly separating Edna from the class of consumptive female protagonists in nineteenth-century novels who waste away and die for love. Edna's animality is more than an expression of her appetites; it is a symbolic embodiment of her assertion of selfhood. To borrow Higonnet's terms, the masculinization of her personality predicts the masculinization of her death.

To this point in this chapter, the discussion has centered on nineteenth-century writers, whereas Sylvia Plath is, of course, a contemporary writer. However, in the most significant areas, Plath's situation is not substantially different from Chopin's. Certainly, the puritanical 1950s in America were primarily informed by the Victorian nineteenth-century, and Plath, in particular, seems very Victorian in her obsession with her body and with physical purity. Plath's own suicide resembles the fictional one of Anna Karenina in Plath's feelings of ambivalence and her yielding to overwhelming social pressures. Plath also resembles Madame Bovary in her obsession with the popular culture myths of romantic love and motherhood. However, the persona that appears in Plath's *Ariel*, and especially in "Edge," which was composed immediately before Plath's suicide, is portrayed as resolved and heroic in her acceptance of death.

Irving Howe, in his comments concerning suicide as a prevailing theme in Sylvia Plath's poetry, asks:

> Suicide is an eternal possibility of our life and therefore always interesting; but what is the relation between a sensibility so deeply captive to the idea of suicide and the claims and possibilities of human existence in general? (15)

In the case of human existence in general for women, perhaps Howe is answered somewhat by Alicia Suskin Ostriker. In *Stealing the Language: The Emergence of Women's Poetry in America*, Ostriker states:

> At the core of the women's poetry movement is the quest for autonomous self–definition. Shaping that quest is a heritage, external and internal, which opposes female autonomy. "If we don't name ourselves we are nothing," says Audre Lorde. "If the world defines you it will define you to your disadvantage." (59)

The suicides that Chopin and Plath portray in their writings are actions in which each character attempts to redefine herself in contrast to societal stereotypes. As Higonnet observes, "To take one's life is to force others to read one's death" (68) and as a consequence to reread that life. Underlying Howe's question is an assumption that suicide is an act primarily of despair and desperation; however, when viewed in the light of the developing feminist consciousness of the late nineteenth and twentieth centuries, suicide has been repoliticized into an existential act of defiance and rebellion.

Another important point that Higonnet establishes that will be useful in analyzing Chopin and Plath's work is that men and women attach very different intents and meanings to the act of suicide: "both in fact and in literature women perceive their own suicides in ways that could be described as visionary rather than violent" (78). Higonnet's observation is clearly exemplified by *The Awakening*. Unlike the other novels discussed in this introduction, in the conclusion of *The Awakening*, the focus remains on Edna. Her death is purely visionary. As Higonnet notes, the novel "fades into a dream-like engulfment of consciousness by the waves of the past" (80). As we shall see, Chopin and Plath are very similar in their approach to the visionary suicide. Both have their characters regress at the moment of death into their childhoods, which represents for them an escape into an idyllic state where all things again become possible. The significance of this motif in woman's writings is summarized by Nina Auerbach in "Falling Alice, Fallen Women, and Victorian Dream Children." Auerbach states, "In the ideology of Victorian womanhood, marriage signaled not maturity but death into a perpetual nursery. Thus, paradoxically, the intact child is in securest possession of the mobility and power of her potential adult future" (52–53). In other words, because of the limiting stereotypical roles that society forces on women, adult sexuality and relationships are a prison for them. In comparison, the only time in her life in which a woman enjoys some autonomy and freedom of choice is during her childhood. This idea that marriage and motherhood for the mature woman are the death of the autonomous self is evident in the conclusion of *The Awakening* when Edna realizes that she would sacrifice everything for her children but herself, by which she means her "self." Edna is forced to the conclusion that, unfortunately, once a woman has embraced her adult sexuality, personal autonomy is no longer available to her, at least not available to her in life. As Higonnet states, "The only way for a woman to attain a state of wholeness may be to move beyond the body" (79), a point of departure on which Chopin and Plath would have agreed. Thus, unlike Tolstoy, Flaubert, and Wharton, Chopin and Plath find in suicide a way to move beyond the body, and they present suicide positively in their works as a form of feminist self-definition.

CHAPTER II

Kate Chopin's Rebel With A Cause:
Edna Pontellier In *The Awakening*

Today, Kate Chopin is considered to be a mainstream American author, and her short stories are regularly anthologized in college textbooks. Her short novel, *The Awakening*, has become required reading in many women's literature courses; however, this has not always been the case. According to Kenneth Eble in his landmark 1956 article "A Forgotten Novel," "When Kate Chopin's novel *The Awakening* was published in 1899, it made its mark on American letters principally in the reactions it provoked among shocked newspaper reviewers" (7). Already a well-known writer of local color short stories when she wrote *The Awakening*, Chopin did not set out to write a controversial novel. In writing the novel, she was attempting to deal at length with the themes of female individuality and sexuality that had already dominated her publicly successful short fiction.

However, that was not the view taken of *The Awakening* in 1899 when it was published. In her preface to the Norton critical edition of the novel, Margaret Culley echoes Eble's statement saying that Chopin's book

> met with widespread hostile criticism and the book was removed from the library shelves in St. Louis. Chopin herself was refused membership in the St. Louis Fine Arts Club because of the novel. In 1906 it was reprinted by Duffield (New York); but then it went out of print and remained so for more than half a century in this country. (vii)

According to tradition, Chopin was crushed by the novel's reception and her subsequent social ostracism in her native St. Louis, and she quit writing and then died a few years later in 1904. Larzer Ziff suggests that the tradition is close to the truth:

> Kate Chopin was not merely rejected, she was insulted. "She was broken-hearted," her son Felix said, and in the remaining five years of her life she produced only a few pieces, although her friends insisted that she still had a great deal to say. (305)

Although Eble points out that the story that Chopin completely stopped writing after the hostile reception to *The Awakening* "is false—her manuscript collection shows that she wrote six stories after 1900," he goes on to agree that "the implications are probably accurate" (7).

Like one of her own strong-willed heroines, Chopin did not simply retreat from the critical attacks. In July 1899 she published the following ironic "retraction" in *Book News*, a literary journal:

> Having a group of people at my disposal, I thought it might be entertaining (to myself) to throw them together and see what would happen. I never dreamed of Mrs. Pontellier making such a mess of things and working out her own damnation as she did. If I had had the slightest intimation of such a thing I would have excluded her from the company. But when I found out what she was up to, the play was half over and it was then too late. (159)

Chopin may have been attempting to mollify the reaction of her contemporaries by pretending that Edna was damned by her actions and that Chopin had no foreshadowing of the ending of her novel; however, as will become clear in this analysis of *The Awakening*, Chopin from the outset clearly intended the outcome of the novel, portraying Edna as doomed rather than damned. Few novels move with such economy of purpose to a consistently foreshadowed conclusion.

Following the initial negative reaction to *The Awakening* were fifty years of neglect. The novel only began to receive critical attention again in the United States during the 1950s in response to the work of a French critic, Cyrille Arnavon (Culley "Editor's Note" 143). Critical recognition in the early Sixties culminated with a piece by Edmund Wilson in 1962 that placed the novel in the American canon: Wilson stated that it "anticipates D. H. Lawrence in its treatment of infidelity" (qtd. in Culley 143).

The rediscovery of Chopin's work and its subsequent legitimization by the critical establishment in the Sixties was quickly followed by her canonization by feminist literary critics in the Seventies. Although it is tempting to see Chopin as a conscious forerunner of the recent feminist movement, Culley points out that Chopin "was never a feminist or a suffragist; in fact, she was suspicious of any ideology. She was committed to personal freedom" ("Context" 117). What made her fiction appeal to feminists is that she acted out her call for personal freedom from limitations primarily through woman characters, some of the least free members of society. Culley concludes:

> Though Kate Chopin was not a feminist, and *The Awakening* is not a political novel in the narrow sense of the term, it is important to understand the political and social context in which it appeared. A novel exploring the consequences of personal—particularly sexual—freedom for the married woman, appearing as it did in a decade much preoccupied with the New Woman in its midst, was certain to provoke strong reactions. (119)

Another strong contributor to these negative reactions was the novel's ending, Edna Pontellier's suicide, which pleased neither the conservatives of the 1890s nor the liberals of the 2000s, because the former did not see Edna's death as penitent but defiant and the latter do not see it as necessary at all. In fact, Edna's suicide has become a touchstone for the novel's critical analysis. Culley classifies the ending as one of the novel's major problems ("Preface" viii), and several modern critics see the ending as totally betraying Chopin's characterization of Edna as a strong-willed woman. Ultimately, to make sense of the book, the reader must understand the complex motivations behind Edna's suicide and how the actions of the novel lead inexorably to that conclusion.

Mal d'amour, unrequited love and resultant self-destruction, has been examined in Chapter I, chiefly using Higonnet's terminology. In *Loving with a Vengeance: Mass-Produced Fantasies for Women*, Tania Modleski describes plots typical of popular narrative fiction produced with women as the target audience, one of which "deal[s] with the woman who gave in to the libertine, and at the end of the novel die[s] a penitent and often excruciating death" (17). To the reader used to this paradigm of romantic fiction, the plot of *The Awakening* appears to be of this genre, and the novel often is interpreted by critics as the story of a naive woman awakening to the concept of sexual pleasure and dying because she could not have it all.

For example, Harold Bloom in his introduction to *Kate Chopin: Modern Critical Views* asserts that the novel is centered on Edna's sexual awakening (1), and Kenneth Eble finds, "Quite frankly, the book is about sex" (9), an idea which is echoed by George Spangler:

> Her brief affair with Arobin hardly proves the certainty of a host of future lovers, but it has clearly shown her what is missing from her life; and since she has long

been indifferent to convention and domestic ties, she could well expect to find
someone less shoddy than Arobin and less scrupulous than Robert. (254)

In other words, all Edna needs is sex with the right man, and she can live
happily ever after. An androcentric reading of the novel insists, as Spangler
exemplifies, that Edna's awakening is sexual, and that sex can somehow
provide her with an escape from the futility of existence.

Yet Chopin's view of the significance of sexuality in *The Awakening* is
not very different from that presented by Ernest Hemingway in *The Sun Also
Rises*. At the center of that novel is the character Jake Barnes, whom
Hemingway portrays as sexually impotent due to a wound received during the
First World War. On the surface, Jake's impotency appears to keep him and
Brett Ashley from marrying and presumably living happily ever after.
However, by the conclusion of *The Sun Also Rises*, it is clear to the reader
that Jake's wound is only an outward symbol of the sterility and absurdity of
modern life. *The Sun Also Rises* does not conclude with Jake and Brett killing
themselves as Edna does in *The Awakening*, but the tone and theme of the two
novels are very similar. Yet critics do not propose that if Jake were suddenly
potent again, all of his problems would be resolved, and it is just as ludicrous
to presume that sex alone can resolve Edna's problems.

Critics such as Bloom, Spangler, and Eble fail to understand the full
nature of Edna's awakening, which is nothing short of an awakening to the
true circumstances of existence for a woman shorn of the romantic illusions
that society foists upon her—an existence in which the deck is so stacked
against women that the only true choice left to them is to continue this
oppressive existence or to die. Larzer Ziff rightly concludes that "Edna
Pontellier is trapped between her illusions and the conditions which society
arbitrarily establishes to maintain itself, and she is made to pay" (23). In the
context of Chopin's novel, suicide is not a running away from life but a
running to it. It becomes the only choice available to a woman who has placed
individual dignity and integrity above all else.

Although Bloom states that feminist critics "weakly misread the book"
because "it is anything but feminist in its stance" (1), feminist literary critics
find that Chopin creates a sympathetic character in Edna Pontellier and that
the novel involves us in Edna's struggle—a struggle to find personal freedom
and fulfillment in a social structure that demands female submission. That this
struggle is doomed should not come as a surprise to the reader, since from the

first chapter Chopin consistently foreshadows Edna's inevitable failure and death. While it is true that a central point of interest in the book is Edna's relationships with men, Chopin's focus is not primarily on Edna as a sexually unfulfilled person or as a woman subsequently fulfilled by her sexual relationship with Alcee Arobin. In other words, sex is not at the center of Edna's quest. Rather, this quest is established from the outset as being grounded in the Romantic ideal, the need of the individual ego to assert itself without restraint. In this regard, Bloom sees Chopin as a daughter of Walt Whitman. He states:

> Walt Whitman, one of the roughs, an American, the self of *Song of Myself*, lusts after "the real me" or "me myself" of Walt Whitman. Chopin's heroine, Edna, becomes, as it were, one of the roughs, an American, when she allows herself to lust after her real me, her me myself...Edna, like Walt, falls in love with her own body, and her infatuation with the inadequate Robert is merely a screen for her overwhelming obsession, which is to nurse and mother herself. (2)

Notice Bloom's reference to the need for feminine ministration and validation at the end of this quotation. This need is at the heart of both Edna's and thus the novel's struggle because women have societal and biological limits that prevent them from fulfilling their romantic egos.

Traditionally, the male romantic ego has received external validation through women. It is through their conquest of women that men have seen themselves as freed from the restraints inherent in their humanity. As Camille Paglia states in *Sexual Personae*, "Women have borne the symbolic burden of man's imperfections, his grounding in nature" (11). She adds, "Man, repelled by his debt to a physical mother, created an alternate reality, a heterocosm to give him the illusion of freedom" (9). Thus man has constructed civilization for the purpose of distancing nature and reducing its ability to limit him. In this process, he has constructed a sexist and racist system designed to place him in a position of superiority over women and over other men, who can be designated as flawed, subhuman, or alien. As Virginia Woolf states in *A Room of One's Own*, "Women have served all these centuries as looking-glasses possessing the magic and delicious power of reflecting the figure of man at twice its natural size. Without that power probably the earth would still be swamp and jungle" (35). This power creates for dominant males a sense of superiority and entitlement not just in relationship to the objects of their oppression, but to nature and its power as well. This does not mean that the man actually has power over the arbitrariness and negation of death, but only that he feels that he does and he feels a sense of entitlement and invulnerability. So, for example, a man does not see himself as growing old; what he sees is his wife growing old, and he feels a sense of outrage at her for this betrayal of him. Rather than confront his personal mortality, he simply gets a new, younger wife. In some respects, this enormous sense of ego lies at the heart of the romantic ideal. But for this ideal to function, it needs a sense of entitlement and a way of projecting nature into an opponent he can grapple with.

In order to accomplish this, man has projected nature onto woman and subjugated it in his subjugation of her. However, it becomes very difficult for this philosophical construct to function as intended if it is a woman who is obsessed with the Romantic ideal. Paglia contends:

> Woman does not dream of transcendental or historical escape from natural cycle, since she is that cycle...The more woman aims for personal identity and autonomy, the more she develops her imagination, the fiercer will be her struggle with nature—that is with the intractable laws of her own body. (10)

And this conflict is at the intuitive heart of Chopin's novel and Edna's dilemma. This is why Chopin is not Walt Whitman's daughter as Harold Bloom insists. In the America of the 1890s, she is instead Whitman's wife, experiencing the futility and absurdity of the Romantic ideal. As we shall see later, Edna does not defy nature, but rather is identified with it. Although there is nothing new in identifying women characters in literature with nature, this identification means something very different to Chopin, since she is a woman.

The serene opening of *The Awakening* stands in ironic juxtaposition to the themes and outcome of the novel. Initially, Edna Pontellier seems like the last person who would shortly rebel against society and sacrifice herself for an abstract concept. At the age of twenty-nine, Edna has led a generally pampered and unremarkable upper-class life. The novel opens on Grand Isle, one of only two settings in the novel, and initially focuses on Mr. Pontellier. This focus is so absolute that Edna is known only as his wife, Mrs. Pontellier, for the first three chapters of the book. In delaying Edna's personal entrance into the novel, Chopin effectively recreates the normal external focus of society that sees the wife as an adjunct to her husband, receiving her identify through him. However, careful reading of these first three chapters reveals intimations of Chopin's theme. In her spare style, Chopin tells the reader much about the married life of Mr. and Mrs. Pontellier. As is often noted by critics, Mr. Pontellier thinks of Edna as "a valuable piece of property" (Chopin 4). Although he is a neglectful father—he does not divert himself from his own indulgences to spend time with his sons and forgets his promise to bring them treats—Mr. Pontellier projects this neglectfulness solely upon his wife: "He reproached his wife with her inattention, her habitual neglect of the children. If it was not a mother's place to look after children, whose on earth was it?" (7). Mr. Pontellier establishes early on with both Edna and the reader that childrearing is her responsibility.

Although he likes to maintain the fiction that Edna is "the sole object of his existence" (7), he demands that he be the sole object of hers. This is subtly demonstrated by two parallel scenes that Chopin sets up in the first few chapters of the novel. Earlier in the day, Edna has had some adventure at the beach that Mr. Pontellier considers to be "utter nonsense," and he cuts her off when she begins to relate her escapade. However, late that evening when he returns from a night out to find his wife sound asleep, he is piqued that she shows "so little interest in things which concerned him and valued so little his conversation" (7). Although Edna does not expect or demand external validation of her identity and importance, her husband does, and he feels it is her responsibility to provide this. To exert his power and control over her, he rouses Edna from her sound sleep over an imagined illness of one of the children, while he, in turn, goes to sleep himself. Chopin portrays Edna as concluding this interaction with her "devoted" husband in tears.

In Chapter IV the theme of Edna's inadequacy as a mother is further explored. Although Edna has not overtly failed in her motherly duty, according to Mr. Pontellier, she does not have the proper attitude. Chopin sums the situation up, saying:

> In short, Mrs. Pontellier was not a mother-woman. The mother-women seemed to prevail that summer at Grand Isle. It was easy to know them, fluttering about with extended, protecting wings when any harm, real or imaginary, threatened their precious brood. They were women who idolized their children, worshiped their husbands, and esteemed it a holy privilege to efface themselves as individuals and grow wings as ministering angels. (10)

Although society held up the image of Coventry Patmore's Angel in the House as the ideal woman, Chopin is not here endorsing it because the key word in this paragraph is *efface*, which connotes a degrading and unrealistic social role. Chopin substitutes for the image of the Angel in the House more natural winged creatures, the various bird images which abound in the novel. And interestingly, Chopin's birds, which symbolize a woman's spirit—in this case Edna's—are presented as caged like the parrot at the beginning of the novel or maimed like the bird flying with the handicap of a broken wing at the end of the novel.

Thus, Chopin begins the novel in a dispassionate, understated manner, showing us Mrs. Pontellier from the perspective of how her husband and society view her. In the sense that Edna has been indoctrinated with this view, it is how she sees herself. It is against this backdrop that we watch Edna's growth as an individual and her actions of attempted rebellion. In Chapter I of this work, I explored the concept of the angel and monster as two standard characterizations of women. Sandra Gilbert and Susan Gubar in *The Madwoman in the Attic* state that it is necessary for the development of the woman artist that both the angel and monster be killed, and Chopin's novel focuses on Edna as she attempts to kill off the false identities of the angel and monster that imprison her in an effort to substitute in their place a third, integrated and true identity, a struggle we shall see repeated in the works of Sylvia Plath.

Despite the fact that I have referred to Mrs. Pontellier as Edna, the reader does not know her first name until Chapter VI, for she has been referred to rather stiltedly as Mrs. Pontellier until then. Obviously, Chopin would not have done this without a rhetorical purpose. It seems even stranger when we note that Edna's physical appearance is fully described in Chapter III. Chopin, in a style typical of the nineteenth-century male writers discussed in the previous chapter, has presented Edna as she would be judged by society and by her external appearance, which society has held up as being so important for a woman. This stylistic device further emphasizes the irony and futility of Edna's subsequent struggle as an individual. Like Tennyson's Lancelot viewing the Lady of Shallott, we can imagine society collectively looking at her dead body at the conclusion of the novel and saying, "She has a pretty face," a judgment that diminishes her struggle.

The irony underlying Chopin's external presentation of Edna in these first few chapters becomes apparent when the reader finally learns Edna's first name and gains insight into her personal thoughts in Chapter VI. In this pivotal chapter—one of the most important in the novel—Chopin shifts her focus from an external and objective view of Edna to the internal and subjective: what is going on inside her mind. The reader soon receives clues that Edna is not yet fully aware of the turmoil developing within her internal, mental and emotional landscape. Chopin begins the chapter by saying that Edna has "two contradictory impulses which impelled her" (14). As Chopin often does in the novel, she implies here both an obvious and immediate meaning and an ultimate, metaphorical one. Literally, Chopin is referring in this chapter to the choice Edna must make to go swimming or not to go swimming with Robert. But symbolically and ultimately, she is referring to Hamlet's existential choice to be or not to be. Chopin writes, "In short, Mrs. Pontellier was beginning to realize her position in the universe as a human being, and to recognize her relations as an individual to the world within and about her" (14-15). Try as she might, as the novel progresses Edna will not be able to reconcile her inner world with the outward demands of society.

Chapter VI also introduces the sea as a major unifying image of the novel. As Eble notes, "The sea, the sand, the sun and sky of the Gulf Coast become almost a presence themselves in the novel. Much of the sensuousness of the book comes from the way the reader is never allowed to stray far from the water's edge" (12). And the sea is an apt feminine image. Paglia notes the affinity when she states, "Woman's body is a sea acted upon by the month's lunar wave motion" (11). Through the course of the novel, Edna develops a special relationship with the sea that is both the symbol of her awakening and the instrument of her death. In a key passage of foreshadowing in Chapter VI, Chopin portrays the sea as a siren calling to Edna's soul.

> The voice of the sea is seductive; never ceasing, whispering, clamoring, murmuring, inviting the soul to wander for a spell in abysses of solitude; to lose itself in mazes of inward contemplation.
> The voice of the sea speaks to the soul. The touch of the sea is sensuous, enfolding the body in its soft, close embrace. (15)

Interestingly, this last sentence appears verbatim at the end of the book in Chapter XXXIX when Edna wades out into the sea to drown herself.

Certainly no accident, the repetition of this exact sentence in these two crucial scenes emphasizes the role the sea plays in the novel, but it also clearly suggests that Edna's awakening is fated to end in death. Chapter VI occurs before Edna develops her romantic infatuation with Robert, before she meets and becomes involved with Alcee Arobin, before any of the major plot developments of the novel occur. This structure underscores Chopin's fundamental pessimism: events and actions will not save Edna, implying that for a woman, ignorance just might be bliss, or might at least ensure her survival. Chopin is highlighting a fundamental contradiction that while for a man self-discovery is both expected and rewarded, a woman can expect the opposite results. Chopin's fatalistic view in the novel echoes that of the Greek tragedians, where the more the protagonist struggles to avert his fate, the more surely he seals it. According to Gilbert and Gubar,

> The cycle of her [the female protagonist's] fate seems inexorable. Renouncing "contemplative purity," she must now embark on that life of "significant action" which, for a woman, is defined as a witch's life because it is so monstrous, so unnatural. (*The Madwoman in the Attic* 42)

Chopin's fatalism can also be classified, like that of other writers of her day, as Naturalistic, or compatible with the philosophy of literary Naturalism. In Edna's case, biology is destiny. However, the reader of *The Awakening* does not have to wait until Chapter VI to receive some subtle clues that all is not well in the seemingly serene paradise of Grand Isle. Chapter I opens with a caged bird, a parrot, unceasingly uttering the refrain in French, "Go away! Go away! For God's sake!" and, as Culley observes in a note to the text, in the background music is being played from an opera that includes a lover's death at sea (4). Thus even casual references, which at first seem to be in the novel for naturalistic color, contribute to its mood.

If Edna experiences one kind of awakening in Chapter VI, the awakening to her true status in life, she experiences another in Chapter VII. Chopin portrays Edna as more emotionally repressed and naive than sexually oppressed:

> Mrs. Pontellier was not a woman given to confidences, a characteristic hitherto contrary to her nature. Even as a child she had lived her own small life all within herself. At a very early period she had apprehended instinctively the dual life— that outward existence which conforms, the inward life which questions. (15)

But as Chopin says, this summer Edna is learning to "loosen…the mantle of reserve that had enveloped her" (15), and she begins that process not with a man but with a woman, Adele Ratignolle, the earth mother of Grand Isle. Ultimately, Edna's most significant relationships in *The Awakening* are with Adele and Mademoiselle Reisz; they are the primary instruments of Edna's various levels of awakening, rather than with the men who are the objects of her projected longings. Only Adele and Reisz have true insight into Edna's struggle.

This is exactly the point that Kathleen Margaret Lant makes in "The Siren of Grand Isle: Adele's Role in *The Awakening*" when she states:

> Most critics…emphasize the role of Leonce Pontellier, Robert Lebrun, and Alcee Arobin in Edna's awakening. Per Seyersted says, for example, that "It is of course Edna's three men who serve as the real catalysts for her double awakening" to both her intellectual and sensuous nature. Kenneth Eble insists that Robert alone first moves Edna: "Robert Lebrun is the young man who first awakens, or rather, is present at the awakening of Edna Pontellier into passion." Such assertions proceed from a male-centered approach to the work, which does not allow that Edna, as a woman, could be stirred by other than a man, and from a failure to read the novel as Chopin has written it. (115)

The importance of this focus on the female characters in the novel to its overall theme is that it refutes the idea that Edna kills herself for love.

If the reader reads the novel as Chopin wrote it, then Adele Ratignolle emerges as one of two primary people, both female, contributing to the changes in Edna. As Chopin clearly states in Chapter VII:

> There may have been—there must have been—influences, both subtle and apparent, working in their several ways to induce her to do this; but the most obvious was the influence of Adele Ratignolle. The excessive physical charm of the Creole had first attracted her, for Edna had a sensuous susceptibility to beauty. Then the candor of the woman's whole existence, which every one might read, and which formed so striking a contrast to her own habitual reserve—this might have furnished a link. Who can tell what metals the gods use in forging the subtle bond which we call sympathy, which we might as well call love. (15)

It is for Adele that Edna first feels the stirrings of love that have eluded her thus far in marriage and motherhood, and it is to Adele that she confides something of her secret mental life. This relationship, which is introduced in Chapter VII right after the lyrical portrayal of the sea, juxtaposes the two images, so that, as Lant points out, Adele is "a human counterpart to the seductive sea that beckons to Edna's soul" (115).

Lant also states that in Chapter VII "Edna begins, with Adele as her muse and guide, to explore the inner life, which she has never experienced fully" (116). When Adele asks Edna "Of whom—of what are you thinking?" (Chopin 17) while they are talking on the beach, Edna begins to explore and verbalize that inner landscape that had been hidden for so long even from herself. Edna divulges a key image in her early life of walking through a limitless meadow of tall grass, an image, which like many other images in this circular novel, will recur in the final chapter. As a young child, Edna was literally running away from her prayers, but metaphorically she was and is running away from societal expectations. As Adele asks, "And have you been running away from prayers ever since, *ma chere?*" (18). Edna confesses that "sometimes I feel this summer as if I were walking through the green meadow again; idly, aimlessly, unthinking and unguided" (18), and in fact she is. But as Lant notes, by the end of this chapter, "Edna is stimulated to look within and to question seriously" (116) the assumptions of her life. Chopin says that with marriage and motherhood, Edna had blindly assumed a role that fate had not fitted her for and from which she had to escape. Her open relationship with Adele is the first step:

> She had put her head down on Madame Ratignolle's shoulder. She was flushed and felt intoxicated with the sound of her own voice and the unaccustomed taste of candor. It muddled her like wine, or like a first breath of freedom. (20)

Note here the sensualness of the description which reinforces the concept that Edna's awakening is not primarily instigated by her relationships with men.

Adele, however, is not a role model for Edna in her struggle. Adele is the supreme mother-woman, and in her way, she is mothering her friend Edna as another in her brood. Adele epitomizes the traditional feminine role that Edna is rejecting for herself as too confining, and this rejection is the source of some friction between the two women. Later in the novel, Edna visits her friend at home with her husband and family, and as she leaves, Chopin concludes:

> Edna felt depressed rather than soothed after leaving them. The little glimpse of

domestic harmony which had been offered her, gave her no regret, no longing. It was not a condition of life which fitted her, and she could see in it but an appalling and hopeless ennui. She was moved by a kind of commiseration for Madame Ratignolle,—a pity for that colorless existence which never uplifted its possessor beyond the region of blind contentment, in which no moment of anguish ever visited her soul, in which she would never have the taste of life's delirium. (56)

Edna is embracing the life of significant action that Gilbert and Gubar discuss, although she does not realize yet that for women this life can often result in their destruction. Lant observes that all of the characters in *The Awakening* represent alternative selves from which Edna can choose, but to choose one would mean the exclusion of the others. She concludes:

Edna's predicament is not uniquely feminine. What she experiences is a universal human longing to divest the authentic self of the false selves that stifle it. None of the selves available to Edna is enough; each involves a renunciation of another part of Edna vital to her existence. Edna's greatest freedom comes in her ability to give these false selves up, to desist from her characteristically feminine way of coping with them—by means of hiding the real and revealing the false selves—and to live, if necessary, in solitude. (122)

What is uniquely feminine about Edna's plight is the restrictive either/or choices that are available to women. To choose one is to forever close the door on others. Ultimately, solitude is just another of these drastic and unrealistic alternatives dictated by an inflexible society.

As numerous critics have noted, Edna also has several significant relationships with male characters in the novel, the first and most important of which is with Robert Lebrun, and it is in Chapter VIII that the reader learns a great deal more about him. Robert is the son of Madame Lebrun, the owner of the resort on Grand Isle where the Pontelliers are staying. Each summer, in the best chivalric tradition, Robert, who is in his mid-twenties, picks out one of the woman visitors to devote himself to, and this summer it is Edna:

He lived in her shadow during the past month. No one thought anything of it. Many had predicted that Robert would devote himself to Mrs. Pontellier when he arrived. Since the age of fifteen, which was eleven years before, Robert each summer at Grand Isle had constituted himself the devoted attendant of some fair dame or damsel. Sometimes it was a young girl, again a widow; but as often as not it was some interesting married woman. (Chopin 12)

In this passage, Chopin hints at Robert's inability to make commitments to women and to follow through with his intentions. Robert is portrayed as the perennially adolescent male. For example, Chopin states that Robert "was always intending to go to Mexico, but some way never got there" (6).

After their shared confidences in Chapter VII, Adele senses the danger inherent in Robert's romantic attentions to the emotionally-receptive Edna. As a favor she asks him to desist in his attentions towards Edna, stating, "She is not one of us; she is not like us. She might make the unfortunate blunder of taking you seriously" (21). However, Robert has no intention of backing away from his involvement with Mrs. Pontellier, a relationship which he portrays as of the noblest kind, and he defends his behavior by comparing himself favorably to Alcee Arobin, a notorious rake who gossip says has been the seducer of several married women. This is the first mention of Arobin in the novel, and interestingly, Robert introduces him to make the point that he is not like Arobin; he is not a victimizer of women. Of course by the end of the novel, it becomes apparent that he is.

By Chapter IX the reader is aware that Edna is unhappy in her marriage and ripe to be seduced by the attentions of Robert Lebrun, which, as has been noted before, would be the alpha and omega of the plot of a standard women's novel. But the reader has also learned that Edna wants experiences that are not commonly available to a woman. In Chapter IX we meet the other important female figure in the novel, Mademoiselle Reisz, who serves as a second potential role model for Edna. Mademoiselle Reisz is an artist who has sacrificed everything else in life for her individual talent. Mademoiselle Reisz is also at Grand Isle this summer and has apparently taken a special liking to Edna as a kindred soul. Chopin writes of Reisz, "She was a disagreeable little woman, no longer young, who had quarreled with almost every one, owing to a temper which was self-assertive and a disposition to trample upon the rights of others" (26). As Lant points out, Reisz has completely rejected for herself the traditional feminine role. She was not and did not strive to be sexually alluring to men: "She was a homely woman, with a small weazened face and body and eyes that glowed. She had absolutely no taste in dress, and wore a batch of rusty black lace with a bunch of artificial violets pinned to the side of her hair" (26). Chopin portrays her as habitually wearing this same outfit whenever she appears in the novel. Lant concludes:

Mademoiselle Reisz is herself without passion. She does not swim, does not immerse herself in experience, and she is without appetite and desire: "She habitually ate chocolates for their sustaining quality; they contained much nutriment in small compass, she said." (121)

Just like Adele, Reisz is an influence on Edna's awakening. She consents to play at Edna's request at a Saturday night fete on the isle, and the instrument she seems to play is Edna herself. As the music played, "the very passions themselves were aroused with her [Edna's] soul, swaying it, lashing it, as the waves daily beat upon her splendid body. She trembled, she was choking, and the tears blinded her" (27). This scene parallels closely the one in Chapter VII with Adele. Strong emotions are stirred in Edna by her developing relationships with both women, but she still has other avenues to explore in her quest.

With each influence, Edna learns a little more about some facet of herself. The culmination of her transformation at Grand Isle occurs in Chapter X when Edna finally learns to swim. All summer long she had been attempting to do so but without success. Of course, her inability to swim keeps her from merging with the sea, and symbolically with the various parts of her personality. Having made the breakthrough, Edna immediately wants "to swim far out, where no woman had swum before" (28), to loosen all restrictions and confines of society and revert to nature, to reach "out for the unlimited in which to lose herself" (29). Now Edna too has moved beyond that reciprocity of emotion just as Lily Bart does in *The House of Mirth*. Edna has committed herself to personal freedom.

It is only after the encounters with Adele and Reisz, through the playing of the music, and finally, by learning to swim, that Edna now is fully awakened to the passage of time and the possibilities of life. Given the importance that romance plays in a woman's mental life due to social conditioning, Edna's initial response is to seek satisfaction for her longings in romantic love. As Adele feared, Edna begins to take Robert's attentions seriously, although as usual it is not something that she verbalizes in her contact with Robert: "Neither did Mrs. Pontellier speak. No multitude of words could have been more significant than those moments of silence, or more pregnant with the first-felt throbbings of desire" (31). It is important to remember that one reason Edna felt fond of her husband was that "no trace of passion or excessive and fictitious warmth colored her affection, thereby threatening its dissolution" (20). Desire, passion, and love might all be natural and unavoidable forces in life, but that does not necessarily mean that to Chopin they were positive forces. Rather like the forces of nature, which she metaphorically linked in her short story "The Storm," sexual attraction was a force beyond human control and direction. As the novel progresses, Chopin explores even further the representation of sexual desire and passion as forces very distinct from love, despite the traditional approach of portraying them as one and the same for women.

Immediately after Chapter X where she finally learns to swim, Edna begins her acts of rebellion against the societal stereotypes of marriage and motherhood that are to characterize the remainder of the novel. She refuses to come to bed once the festivities are over that night, although Leonce first entreats, then demands that she do so. For the first time, she sees through Leonce's ploys to control her behavior, telling him, "Don't speak to me like that again; I shall not answer you" (32).

Edna next enjoys a brief romantic interlude with Robert on the island of Cheniere Caminada, away from husband and children and even further away from civilization. It is immediately after this seemingly idyllic day that Robert suddenly and mysteriously decides to actually embark on his long–planned foray to Mexico. His decision comes as a surprise certainly to Edna, but also to the reader, who might have been led to conclude that at this point in the novel Edna would just substitute Lebrun for Pontellier and continue on with life as usual. Although it might appear that Robert finally took Adele's warning seriously and for the sake of Edna did the "right thing" and left, by the end of the novel it becomes quite apparent that Robert fled before an assertive Edna to protect his romantic illusions.

During their visit to Cheniere Caminada, Edna takes charge of the relationship. She summons Robert to go with her, and she puts her desires first during that day. Although Robert, like Leonce Pontellier, likes to maintain the fiction that he is the submissive devotee with women, the woman actually is merely the mirror to his romantic ego, his narcissism. The intrusion of a real and demanding Edna into this romantic construct is unwelcomed. It is interesting to note that after Robert leaves he writes passionately to Mademoiselle Reisz about Edna, but not to Edna herself. In that way, he again relegates Edna to the object, the holy grail, of his romantic quest, without risking having to deal with the demands of a living person; it is obvious that to Robert love and sex are two separate things. He claims as love objects untouchable and unobtainable women that are married, such as Edna, while Chopin hints that he has been sexually involved with the dark maiden, Mariequita.

In this respect Chopin exploits a standard literary motif well documented by Leslie Fiedler in his book *Love and Death in the American Novel.* Fiedler states,

> All through the history of our novel, there had appeared side by side with the Fair Maiden, the Dark Lady—sinister embodiment of the sexuality denied the snow maiden. The Indian...is divided into...good Indian and bad; and similarly woman is bifurcated into Fair Virgin and Dark Lady, the glorious phantom at the mouth of the cave, and hideous Moor who lurks within. In each case, the dark double represents the threat of both sex and death...In such a symbolic world, sex and death become one. (296)

Fiedler goes on to point out that in the sentimental American novel the Fair Maiden was presented as an object "refined to the point where copulation with her seems blasphemous" (293). This is the role that Edna plays in Robert's mythic imagination; however, Robert's is a masculine viewpoint clearly not shared or even perceived by Edna.

With Chapter XVII Chopin switches the scene of the novel to the city of New Orleans. Chopin uses only two settings in the novel, the world of Grand Isle, which is analogous to the Garden of Eden, aligned with nature, and the city of New Orleans, which represents society and civilization with all their arbitrary rules and prejudices. Edna's awakening occurs in nature at Grand Isle, and when she reenters civilization, man's construct against nature, she becomes increasingly frustrated by her quest for autonomy. Only in nature can Edna be free, and the island itself is a metaphor for Edna, who is Chopin's solitary soul (the original title for the novel), surrounded on all sides by water and cut off from community.

The first chapter set in New Orleans bears interesting parallels to the first chapter in the novel, as if Chopin wanted to reemphasize the basic relationship between Leonce and Edna. Again, the materialism of Pontellier is emphasized:

> Mr. Pontellier was very fond of walking about his house examining its various appointments and details, to see that nothing was amiss. He greatly valued his possessions, chiefly because they were his, and derived genuine pleasure from

contemplating a painting, a statuette, a rare lace curtain—no matter what—after he
had bought it and placed it among his household gods. (50)

Since Edna has earlier been characterized as one of Mr. Pontellier's
possessions, this description can apply to her as another kind of object placed
in his house. The reference to "household gods" connotes the idea of Pontellier
as a paterfamilias, which according to the Napoleonic law code of Louisiana,
he very much is. Soon after their return to New Orleans, Mr. Pontellier
departs to New York on business, and Edna now continues her pilgrim's
progress of self-discovery. She next turns to two well-known traditional male
vehicles as antidotes for angst—art and sex.

Early in the novel, Edna exhibits some talent as a painter, and she now
pursues it as a full-time occupation, turning inward to express herself as an
existential human being through art. In this enterprise, Mademoiselle Reisz
acts as both her mentor and as a warning of what Edna could become,
because the existence that Reisz encourages Edna to embrace is isolating and
solitary. Mademoiselle Reisz attempts to point these consequences out to Edna
in telling her: "The bird that would soar above the level plain of tradition and
prejudice must have strong wings. It is a sad spectacle to see the weaklings
bruised, exhausted, fluttering back to earth" (82). Ultimately, Edna's wings
are not that strong.

Actually, Edna appears in the novel as a character on a continuum
between Adele Ratignolle and Mademoiselle Reisz. She has children like
Adele but cannot find fulfillment or even acquiescence in a biologically
determined role that strips her of her individuality. Yet she cannot embrace the
other societal choice open to her, that of the neutered female hermit, the
spinster, Mademoiselle Reisz. Although Edna rejects the traditional female
role, she does not reject her sexuality but rather embraces it, as is
demonstrated by the many scenes where Chopin has her admiring her own
body. Carley Rees Bogarand in "*The Awakening*: A Refusal to Compromise"
observes, "At first Edna's decision to begin a new life as artist seems to free
her, but she learns that she cannot be both a sexual person and a successful
person" (17). Since, as Camille Paglia concludes, art is a male construct to
distance and control nature, such a construct would not work for a woman:

The Greek pattern of free will to *hybris* to tragedy is a male drama, since woman
has never been deluded (until recently) by the mirage of free will. She knows there

is no free will, since she is not free. She has no choice but acceptance. Whether she desires motherhood or not, nature yokes her into the brute inflexible rhythm of procreative law. (10)

Nonetheless, having awakened to the "beauty and brutality" (Chopin 83) that constitutes existence, Edna refuses to compromise and, therefore, kills herself.

However, in her quest for freedom, before reaching that final conclusion, Edna pursues one other potential avenue of escape—sex. She is following a time-honored male tradition here, in investing adultery with the capacity to provide meaning to life and to keep one forever young, staving off death and decline. From time to time in the novel, the reader has heard about the escapades of the rake, Alcee Arobin. Edna meets him upon her return to New Orleans, and he begins to pursue her. Chopin describes him as being rather superficial: "He possessed a good figure, a pleasing face, not overburdened with depth of thought or feeling; and his dress was that of the conventional man of fashion" (74). When Arobin is ultimately successful in his goal of sexual conquest, Edna realizes that love and sex are often separate. She reflects on the encounter: "There was a dull pang of regret because it was not the kiss of love which had inflamed her, because it was not love which had held this cup of life to her lips" (83). To Edna, sex without love is ultimately unsatisfying, and Arobin influences her least of all. She has more of an effect on him than he does on her, for he continues the pursuit after she is no longer interested.

Finally, Edna tries one more time to integrate the disparate elements of her life when Robert returns to New Orleans. Interestingly, he makes no attempt to contact her, preferring still to worship her from afar. His hesitancy confuses Edna, and she never seems to fully comprehend Robert's perception of her. When they are accidentally reunited, it is Edna who responds with passion: "She took his face between her hands and looked into it as if she would never withdraw her eyes more. She kissed him on the forehead, the eyes, the cheeks, and the lips" (106). If this display of passion were not enough to cause Robert's rapid retreat, then her announcement of emancipation that follows surely would and does. Attempting to reassure Robert that she is free to pursue a relationship with him, she states, "I am no longer one of Mr. Pontellier's possessions to dispose of or not. I give myself where I choose" (106-7). This statement, of course, is the last thing Robert wants to hear. It is at this climactic point in the novel that Edna is summoned to assist Adele with the impending birth of her baby, and Robert makes good his escape, leaving an inadequate note saying, "I love you. Good-by—because I love you" (111).

At the beginning of the novel, the reader learned that Adele Ratignolle is once again pregnant, and references to the development of the fetus, which appear throughout the novel provide a subtle metaphor for the development of Edna's growing individuality. Despite the fact that she already has had several children, Adele still shows dread of the birth process, and she forces from Edna a promise to help her when she has the baby. Keeping that commitment, Edna leaves Robert to go to Adele; however, Adele's delivery is extremely unpleasant for Edna. Although Edna has had two children herself, she can only recall the experience as "an ecstasy of pain, the heavy odor of chloroform, a stupor which had deadened sensation, and an awakening to find a new life to which she had given being, added to the great unnumbered multitude of souls that come and go" (108-09). In other words, she really has no clear recollection of the childbirth experience. But now that she is an observer of the delivery, rather than a participant in it, the experience affects her profoundly:

> She began to wish she had not come; her presence was not necessary. She might have invented a pretext for staying away; she might even invent a pretext now for going. But Edna did not go. With an inward agony, with a flaming, outspoken revolt against the ways of Nature, she witnessed the scene [of] torture. (109)

Here, Edna is confronted with the biological limits to personal freedom for women that cannot be transcended. It remains only for her to fully realize the implications of her epiphany, a task in which Dr. Mandelet assists just as he assisted in the birth of Adele's baby.

Throughout the novel, Dr. Mandelet, as the wise old doctor, has been called upon to dispense advice to various characters. In that role, when the ordeal is over Dr. Mandelet walks Edna home, and in a speech intended to comfort her, he instead crystallizes the crux of her dilemma:

> The trouble is…that youth is given up to illusions. It seems to be a provision of Nature; a decoy to secure mothers for the race. And Nature takes no account of moral consequences, of arbitrary conditions which we create, and which we feel obliged to maintain at any cost. (109–10)

In this passage, Chopin is using Dr. Mandelet to talk directly to her audience, summing up the theme of the novel. Nature is arbitrary and beyond our control, and it often makes a mockery of the society and civilization that we have built up to control and contain it. Nature may not be good, but it is real and cannot be ignored. As Lant concludes on this theme and its relationship to Adele Ratignolle's role in the novel:

> Appropriately, Adele Ratignolle, who siren-like first enticed Edna to her journey in the sea, is the agent responsible for her destruction in the sea. Called to Adele's confinement, Edna witnesses the birth of Adele's child, and she recalls her own lying-in with fear and horror. Giving birth is the ultimate sleep, the final giving up of will. (123)

Paglia reaches a similar conclusion concerning the experience of childbirth for a woman, calling it "nature's heart of darkness...The so-called miracle of birth is nature getting her own way" (11). Having looked into this "heart of darkness," Edna returns to Grand Isle, wanders down to the beach ostensibly for a swim, but instead, engages in her ultimate act of rebellion by swimming out to sea and presumably drowning.

Though Edna may have appeared up to this point to be wandering aimlessly on her voyage of self-discovery, actually, in retrospect, she has been systematically exploring the various concepts that are supposed to give purpose to human existence. Family, love, art, and sex—all are explored by Edna and ultimately rejected as trapping rather than freeing women, because each of these concepts is predicated on the idea of manipulating women. Bogarand asserts that Edna "remains unsatisfied because all of the choices available to her are destructive" (25).

On the beach at Grand Isle, Edna has her final awakening. As she tells Adele earlier in the novel, "she would give up the unessential, but she would never sacrifice herself for her children" (113). Now, at Grand Isle, Edna realizes the full consequences of that statement: "The children appeared before her like antagonists who had overcome her; who had overpowered and sought to drag her into the soul's slavery for the rest of her days. But she knew a way to elude them" (113)—that way being suicide. Lant concludes:

> Edna realizes...[that] the only way to renounce biology is to renounce the physical self. She has given up the dual life of secrecy, conformity, and lies, which

concealed her questions and assertiveness. She has tossed off the garments of false selves; she has learned to swim, to master the waves and move away from the shore to freedom. But she cannot renounce her sons; she can only "elude them," and she must give up the body to elude her sons. In so doing she must lose the self. (123)

John May in his study of local color in the novel echoes Lant's conclusion:

The ultimate realization that she has awakened to is that the only way she can save herself is to give up her life. She cannot accept the restrictions that nature and man have conspired to impose upon her, the perpetual frustration of desire that living entails. And so, paradoxically, she surrenders her life in order to save herself. (195)

The symbolic relationship that Chopin develops between Edna and the sea carries through to her suicide, a relationship that has several symbolic meanings. In reality, drowning is a preferred method for women to commit suicide. In her book *Victorian Suicide*, Barbara Gates finds that "In most cases, women chose poison or drowning over bloodier deaths by gun or knife, a pattern which continues today" (125). Olive Anderson in *Suicide in Victorian and Edwardian England* also reports "the much greater use women made of drowning as a method of suicide," adding that "'found drowned' was a recognized euphemism for female suicide" (43). Death by drowning usually allowed the victim and her family to escape the stigma that was attached to the suicide and the negative legal consequences:

Since there was often no clear evidence of how the body came to be in the water, and in law sudden death was presumed accidental until proved otherwise, a verdict of suicide was easily avoided in drowning cases—at least until coroners increasingly led their juries to accept circumstantial evidence on the point. It has been argued, moreover, that families always have a greater incentive to conceal female suicide; and it is not improbable that in cases of doubt there was often greater readiness to avoid verdicts of suicide on women. (44)

One can imagine the very similar interpretation that Pontellier and his circle would have put on Edna's suicide. She too would have been labeled "found drowned," her death called an accident that might have resulted from her recent evident mental instability.

Death by drowning also developed a symbolic meaning in the literature and art of the nineteenth century. Gates calls drowning a "female-associated type of death" representative of "dissolution into a body of water" (135). Not only was drowning a preferred method of suicide for women, but it was the preferred method for artists and writers to portray female suicide. Some examples include the Pre-Raphaelite paintings "Found Drowned" by George Frederic Watts and "Ophelia" by John Everett Millais, Thomas Hood's poem "The Bridge of Sighs," George Eliot's *The Mill on the Floss*, and Stephen Crane's *Maggie: A Girl of the Streets*. Gates humorously asserts that "Dickens presented a phalanx of fallen women moving towards the Thames" (135).

Probably the best-known literary figure who commits suicide by drowning is Ophelia in Shakespeare's *Hamlet*, a play with parallel threads of male and female madness and death. Feminist critic Elaine Showalter maintains that Ophelia is a major prototype for the madwoman figure in art and literature: "The stage conventions associated with the role have always emphasized the feminine nature of Ophelia's insanity as contrasted with Hamlet's universalized metaphysical distress" (11). She adds:

All of these conventions carried dual messages about femininity and insanity. The woman with her hair down indicated an offense against decorum, and improper sensuality. Ophelia's flowers, too, came from the Renaissance iconography of female sexuality; in giving them away, she symbolically "deflowers" herself. Even her death by drowning has associations with the feminine and the irrational, since water is the organic symbol of woman's fluidity: blood, milk, tears. (11)

The Awakening concludes with images of both water and flowers—the sea and "the musky odor of pinks" (Chopin 114), or dianthus.

Many critics have noted the association of woman with water, corresponding to her mythical identification with the moon that controls the tides and, in romantic thought, woman's nature. Gates echoes Showalter in concluding:

It was as though women drowned in their own tears, or returned to the water of the womb, or, as Freud believed, were delivered of a child when they made their final retreat into water. Fallen women thus drowned in grief or in conjunction with childbearing, both of which were associated with their state and with female fluids in general. (135)

In the works of many artists, male and female, water becomes not only the means of the woman's death, but a symbol in the work of her fallen state and a predictor of her necessary end. Gates points out, "In Victorian literature, many fallen women openly acknowledged this affinity with water" (135), which is an acknowledgement of their destiny and eventual end. As has been discussed, Edna's awakening is brought on early in the novel partially by her baptism at sea when she learns how to swim. By learning to swim, she learns to take action and to express her self-will, which Thomas Carlyle in *Sartor Resartus* maintains is the only barrier man had against suicide (Gates 29). However, as has already been demonstrated, what works for a man, often works to the detriment of a woman. It is this very action and self-will that paradoxically lead to her demise.

There are two scenes in the novel that concentrate on Edna's integration with the sea—when Edna first learns to swim and when she commits suicide, and a close comparison of these scenes demonstrates the unity of theme in the novel. As pointed out before, some critics see Edna's awakening as an awakening merely to sexual pleasure, but Chopin clearly links Edna's awakening to an earlier event that represents Edna's assertion of self-will, learning to swim. Edna has been attempting to learn to swim during the whole period she had been at Grand Isle but has evidently lacked the courage necessary to do so: "A certain ungovernable dread hung about her when in the water, unless there was a hand near by that might reach out and reassure her" (28). Suddenly, she breaks through the barriers that have been holding her back and achieves her goal. Her immediate feeling is one of personal triumph:

> that night she was like the little tottering, stumbling, clutching child, who of a sudden realizes its powers, and walks for the first time alone, boldly and with over-confidence. She could have shouted for joy. She did shout for joy, as with a sweeping stroke or two she lifted her body to the surface of the water.
>
> A feeling of exultation overtook her, as if some power of significant import had been given her soul. She grew daring and reckless, overestimating her strength. She wanted to swim far out, where no woman had swum before. (28)

The images used in this passage are central to an understanding of the book, and they are images that appear over and over again in the novel, unifying it. Of course, as the novel progresses, we find Edna being daring and reckless, overestimating her strength. She attempts to exceed the barriers or boundaries placed around women. In the continuation of this important scene, her suicide is in fact clearly foreshadowed by the association of the fallen woman, Edna, with water, just as Gates has documented. As Edna is swimming, she is "reaching out for the unlimited in which to lose herself" (29); she is attempting to dissolve into the infinity that water represents. But as Edna looks back at the shore and "the people she had left there…a quick vision of death smote her soul, and for a second of time appalled and enfeebled her senses" (29). She even refers to her triumphant swim later as an "encounter with death" (29) because she intuitively realizes that it represents her potential dissolution as a separate individual into the vastness of nature.

The images and tone utilized in the first swimming scene recur precisely in Edna's final scene when she returns to Grand Isle, and seemingly on the spur of the moment decides to kill herself. Since these scenes are so closely parallel in construction, Edna's end has been made necessary by her beginning. In her final scene at Grand Isle, Edna again refers to herself as a child: "How strange and awful it seemed to stand naked under the sky! how delicious! She felt like some new-born creature, opening its eyes in a familiar world that it had never known" (113). As Edna walks out into the water, Chopin writes that she "lifted her white body and reached out with a long, sweeping stroke" (113), repeating the words and images from the first swimming scene. At this time, Edna recalls the terror of her first swim, but she does not look back now. Instead, she finds the sea sensuous and embracing, with no beginning or end, exactly the infinite entity in which she now yearns to lose herself.

As Edna swims, her mind drifts back to her childhood, back to the scene she described to Adele when, long ago on the beach, Adele asked Edna what she was thinking. She remembers her home in Kentucky:

> Edna heard her father's voice and her sister Margaret's. She heard the barking of an old dog that was chained to the sycamore tree. The spurs of the cavalry officer clanged as he walked across the porch. There was the hum of bees, and the musky odor of pinks filled the air. (114)

With this ending, Chopin leaves Edna in a dreamlike trance, a fantasy. By not describing in detail Edna's physical death or its aftermath, Chopin suggests a tone of peace and escape. To apply Higonnet's insights to Edna's suicide, it is presented as visionary rather than violent, and can be interpreted in a completely positive way, allowing the reader to see Edna as finally triumphant rather than defeated. Sandra Gilbert certainly supports this interpretation in "The Second Coming of Aphrodite: Kate Chopin's Fantasy of Desire":

> I think it is possible to argue that Edna's last swim is not a suicide—that is, a death—at all, or, if it is a death, it is a death associated with a resurrection, a pagan, female Good Friday that promises a Venusian Easter. Certainly, at any rate, because of the way it is presented to us, Edna's supposed suicide enacts not a refusal to accommodate the limitations of reality but a subversive questioning of the limitations of both reality and "realism." For, swimming away from the white beach of Grand Isle, from the empty summer colony and the equally empty fictions of marriage and maternity, Edna swims, as the novel's last sentences tell us, not into death but back into her own life, back into her own vision, back into the imaginative openness of her childhood. (57)

That Edna's suicide is misunderstood by some critics is not surprising, considering the hold the romantic paradigm has on the literary depiction of female suicide. In *The Awakening*, Chopin remasculinizes female suicide. Contrary to the conclusions of critics such as George Spangler who feel that the ending does not fit the novel, there is much textual evidence foreshadowing Edna's suicide. Spangler makes his the standard case in "*The Awakening*: A Partial Dissent," stating, ". . . one can easily and happily join in the praise that in recent years has been given to *The Awakening*—one can, that is, until one reaches the conclusion of the novel, which is unsatisfactory because it is fundamentally evasive" (186). Spangler elaborates on what he sees as the problem:

> And what is wrong with this conclusion? Its great fault is inconsistent characterization, which asks the reader to accept a different and diminished Edna from the one developed so impressively before. Throughout the novel the most striking feature of Edna's character has been her strength of will, her ruthless determination to get her own way...Yet in the final pages, Mrs. Chopin asks her reader to believe in an Edna who is completely defeated by the loss of Robert, to believe in the paradox of a woman who has awakened to passional life and yet quietly, almost thoughtlessly, chooses death. (187)

Thus Spangler sees Edna as defeated and destroyed by *mal d'amour*, but he has missed the consistency of symbols and tone throughout the novel that predicts the ending, such as the parallel swimming scenes and the images of the sea at both the beginning and end of the novel. Ultimately, Gilbert and Gubar's general feminist approach is more rewarding. Edna awakens to her situation as a woman, and in her quest for identity through a life of significant action, she must paradoxically choose suicide as the only means available to her to achieve her goal. As Larzer Ziff concludes in *The American 1890s: Life and Times of a Lost Generation* concerning Chopin's message in writing the novel:

> Whether girls should be educated free of illusions, if possible, whether society should change the conditions it imposes on women, or whether both are needed, the author does not say; the novel is about what happened to Edna Pontellier. (304–5)

And in this novel, Edna writes her story with her body.

CHAPTER III

At Ease At The Gate:
Sylvia Plath's *The Bell Jar*

More so than most writers, Sylvia Plath's work has been interpreted in light of her life, chiefly because of her suicide in 1963 at the age of thirty. In the case of the book *Pathways to Suicide: A Survey of Self-Destructive Behaviors* by Ronald W. Maris, the author uses Plath's life as evidenced by her poetry and novel as a case study of deviant behavior. Maris makes no distinction between the events in the life of the writer, Sylvia Plath, and the various personae that appear in Plath's work. Initially, one feels that Maris, a sociologist rather that a literary critic, is literally confusing fact with fiction in his analysis, but ironically, Maris intuitively focuses on one of the key issues of Plath scholarship. Plath critics often treat her work and her life as a seamless web.

This attitude is reflected by A. Alvarez in *The Savage God*, one of the few books written specifically on the subject of suicide and literature. Alvarez was a friend of Plath's, and his book was occasioned by her suicide. Alvarez postulates the following theory behind the theme of Plath's work:

> It is as though she had decided that, for her poetry to be valid, it must tackle head–on nothing less serious than her own death, bringing to it a greater wealth of invention and sardonic energy than most poets manage in a lifetime of so-called affirmation.
> If the road had seemed impassable, she proved that it wasn't. It was, however, one-way, and she went too far along it to be able, in the end, to turn back. Yet her actual suicide...is by the way; it adds nothing to her work and proves nothing about it. It was simply a risk she took in handling such volatile material. (qtd. in Schwartz and Bollas 147)

As several critics have noted, this passage evinces a fundamental misunderstanding of Plath's motives in her writing. The operating concept that Alvarez portrays is that Plath with free will chose the subject matter of death and madness as her personal poetic territory, and for her hubris received the "poetic justice" of dying by her own hand. Jon Rosenblatt in *Sylvia Plath: The Poetry of Initiation* summarizes Alvarez's characterization of Plath: "He presents a romantic view of a poet who heroically pursues the sources of her own inner torment, following Robert Lowell's lead in *Life Studies* (1959), until she is destroyed by her own quest for self-knowledge" (10). Rosenblatt concludes that "Alvarez's view appears to be based on nothing more than a fervent desire to believe in art as a potentially self-destructive and, therefore, existential activity" (11); thus, Alvarez portrays Plath as the Romantic martyr.

Murray Schwartz and Christopher Bollas in "The Absence at the Center: Sylvia Plath and Suicide" also take exception to Alvarez's portrayal, explaining:

> This vision of the poet is perhaps more comforting than Alvarez and others who have carefully explicated the themes and images of "extremist" poets, would wish to admit. He implies the conscious choice of the artist in an obsession with death, minimizes anxiety, and adopts an "as if" tone that can substitute for a searching out of true motives. (147–48)

Schwartz and Bollas contend what should be obvious about confessional poets—one cannot separate their work from their lives. And in the case of Plath in particular, it is clearly fallacious to portray her as a mentally stable individual who metaphorically played with fire in her writings and got burned. Sylvia Plath's work is an outpouring of the grief and despair of a woman who believed too much in the domestic myth of twentieth-century America. Her actual suicide is not separate from her work, but rather her work was an attempt to objectify her experience, to forestall her death.

Irving Howe reflects a better understanding of Plath's point of view, at least in her final poems, when he states:

> The sense of direct speech addressed to an audience is central to confessional writing. But the most striking poems Sylvia Plath wrote are quite different. They are poems written out of an extreme condition, a state of being in which the speaker, for all practical purposes Sylvia Plath herself, has abandoned the sense of audience and cares nothing about—indeed, is hardly aware of—the presence of anyone but herself. (13)

Howe goes on to conclude:

> She exists in some mediate province between living and dying, and she appears to be balancing coolly the claims of the two, drawn almost equally to both yet oddly comfortable with the perils of where she is…at ease at the gate of dying. (13)

The central questions for Howe and other critics are what brought Plath to this gate and what bearing should biography have on interpretation of her work?

Apparently, two biographical influences dominated her life and, therefore, her work: the death of her father shortly after her eighth birthday and the relentless demands of her mother for achievement and perfection, both of which Plath internalized. Otto Plath, Sylvia's father, was a biology professor at Boston University who is principally known for his book *Bumblebees and Their Ways*, which was published in 1934 when Sylvia was two years old. His death in 1940 from the complications of diabetes brought profound changes to Plath's life. Her mother went back to work teaching shorthand and typing at the School for Secretarial Studies at Boston University, her maternal grandparents moved in with her mother in order to take care of the children and to help support the family, and the family moved from the seaside town of Winthrop, Massachusetts, inland to Wellesley. Such a shocking transition to a child of eight would seem a predictor of a very anxious and insecure adulthood, a conclusion which Maris draws when he states, "Sylvia's early trauma led to a very basic and tenacious subjective inadequacy. All of her achievements, straight-A grades, prizes, fellowships, and awards could not substitute for her loss of early love and noncontingent approval" (129).

Added to the sense of loss of father, home, school, and friends that Plath had to contend with was her love-hate relationship with her mother, who, supposedly for Sylvia's own good, relentlessly pushed her to achieve. Plath appears to be the kind of child who did not need much prodding; however, the primary issue is that Plath did not feel that her mother would allow her to make a different choice. In Maris's words, "'Mother love' is freely given, or withheld, without regard to merit; and later achievements, no matter how grand, can never substitute for early noncontingent acceptance" (129). Critics have primarily focused on Plath's relationship with her father in analyzing her work, and in the process have often ignored Sylvia's relationship to her mother. However, in her chapter on Sylvia Plath in *Modern American Women Poets*, Jean Gould explores Plath's relationship with her mother as reflected in her poetry:

> Only one poem, "The Disquieting Muses," portrays Plath's mother, directly, and it is an inadequate maternal figure at first, trying to comfort her children during the disastrous hurricane of 1938, which hit the town of Winthrop with such terrific force that the twelve windows in Professor Plath's study were smashed to pieces; this is followed by a monstrous mother-love, hungry for reflected glory, pushing her daughter into every field of culture with or without talent, forcing her to become an overachiever. Resentment burns beneath every line. The key to the mother-daughter relationship—indeed, the core of her behavior pattern—may be found in

the last lines: "And this is the kingdom you bore me to, / Mother, mother. But no frown of mine / Will betray the company I keep." (128)

Apparently, in order to please her mother, early in her life Plath developed a public mask to hide the unhappy child contained within.

Thus, as Gould points out, during her childhood and adolescent years Plath outwardly appeared to be happy and well-adjusted. She seemed to embrace wholeheartedly the goals of achievement that her mother espoused for her. During this period Plath won numerous academic and literary awards, and Gould says, "Ostensibly, she was the perfect student and all-American adolescent—friendly, outgoing, an earnest worker with creative talent that showed great promise" (129). In some respects, the duality of Plath's nature is reminiscent of Kate Chopin's characterization of Edna Pontellier in *The Awakening*: "Even as a child she had lived her own small life all within herself. At a very early period she had apprehended instinctively the dual life—that outward existence which conforms, the inward life which questions" (15). As is true of many people traumatized in their youth, Plath desperately tried to create a perfect image of herself and her family to cover her underlying sense of loss and abandonment. If Edna was at the top of Maslow's hierarchy of needs, concerned with self-actualization, Plath was at the bottom, obsessed with control and security. Maris states of Plath, "This inability to accept self and others led almost inexorably to social isolation. Plath became intensely, even painfully, critical, compulsive, perfectionistic, and rigid" (130).

The culmination of Plath's frantic quest for achievement during her adolescence came when she was selected to be a guest editor at *Mademoiselle* magazine in New York for the month of June 1953. Although she again seemed to breeze through that experience in characteristic fashion, shortly after she returned from New York, on August 24 of that year, she attempted to kill herself by taking an overdose of sleeping pills and crawling into a secluded portion of the basement of her house. The carefully constructed facade had crumbled, and the remainder of Plath's life was spent in alternately reconstructing this facade and tearing it down again. The events of that summer were the source for her only novel, *The Bell Jar*, written some ten years later in her final frenzied period of writing before her last, and successful, suicide attempt.

Although Plath got her initial literary recognition as a writer of short stories and poetry, her reputation today comes almost exclusively for her poetry. Her only work of sustained prose is *The Bell Jar*, which is consistent in theme and imagery with Plath's poetry, if inferior in execution. The novel "is conspicuously autobiographical" (Smith 33).

Gould theorizes that the instigating force behind Plath's emotional breakdown, an experience that is at the core of the novel, was the usually normal rite of passage of adolescence—the initiation into sexual relationships and the concomitant development of a woman's adult identity. As we have already seen in the preceding chapters, sexual encounters for women are fraught with the possible practical consequences of pregnancy and abandonment and the philosophical consequences of loss of female individuality, consequences that loomed large to the emotionally unstable Plath. Plath's plight was compounded by the prudery of the American 1950s, an era which in many ways was just as restricting for women as the 1890s of Chopin. In Plath's world, women theoretically may have had more opportunities for individual accomplishments, such as attending Smith College and working for *Mademoiselle* magazine, but society still primarily emphasized the roles of wife and mother as the proper choices for women. Obviously, a talented woman such as Plath could easily feel confused by the mixed signals she received from society.

The plot of *The Bell Jar* is substantially the same as the biography just presented. The protagonist, Esther Greenwood (Greenwood was the maiden name of Plath's maternal grandmother who raised her and for whom she had great affection), goes to New York as one of twelve girls selected to be guest editors for *Ladies' Day* magazine. Although this experience should be the high point of Esther's somewhat sheltered life, she finds her reactions to the experience disturbing. As Esther says, "It was my first big chance, but here I was, sitting back and letting it run through my fingers like so much water" (5). Rather than the elation she expected, Esther summarizes her feelings as follows: "I guess I should have been excited the way most of the other girls were, but I couldn't get myself to react. I felt very still and very empty, the way the eye of a tornado must feel, moving dully along in the middle of the surrounding hullabaloo" (3). After she returns from New York, Esther sinks into a full-fledged nervous breakdown for which a male psychiatrist prescribes electro-shock therapy, a common treatment for women at the time. Esther subsequently attempts suicide, just as Plath did, and is institutionalized. The remainder of the novel concerns Esther's stay at several mental hospitals and her development of a reconstructed personality, chiefly with the help of a female psychiatrist, Dr. Nolan. As the novel develops, the gender of Plath's doctors becomes part of the novel's theme. The male psychiatrist, Dr. Gordon, is aloof and self-centered while Dr. Nolan is understanding and helpful.

Esther's relationship with Dr. Nolan is integral to her learning to value her femininity. Esther makes a breakthrough towards the conclusion of the novel when she exclaims, "I don't see what women see in other women," and Dr. Nolan responds, "Tenderness" (246-7). It is this tenderness, which Esther learns from Dr. Nolan that is one of the major ingredients in Esther's eventual recovery.

With such a plot, *The Bell Jar* obviously lends itself to a feminist reading, as do most of Plath's poems. Jon Rosenblatt, however, denies Plath the label of feminist writer. In *Sylvia Plath: The Poetry of Initiation*, he begins by attempting to destroy several misconceptions about Plath's work. The primary misconception to him presents Plath "as a representative female victim in the literature on sexual politics, a casualty of the patriarchal world of marriage and art" (4). He goes on to state:

> In these versions of feminist criticism, Plath is the classic victim of male neglect, male contempt for women, and male chauvinist discrimination. Her death is a form of martyrdom; her life, a case history in the devilish cultural politics that favor men over women and destroy women's creativity. (5)

Rosenblatt dismisses this theory by citing Plath's blazing career as an artist and the many tokens of recognition she received. He concludes, "It is simply inaccurate, then, to invoke the specter of a masculine 'conspiracy' against Plath either during her life or after her death. She did not suffer from a critical or cultural neglect greater than that experienced by male poets in America" (7). He also contends that Plath was not a feminist nor was she overtly political in her work except for some limited examples.

I agree with Rosenblatt on both of these points; however, I do not feel that these are the only, or even most important, ways in which women artists can be oppressed. Plath portrays her source of oppression as stemming from her gender without regard to her role as an artist. Plath was not particularly political in her approach, partially because she predated the political activism of the 1960s and partially as a result of the same phenomenon that Irving Howe recognizes in her work—her lack of interest in audience. Plath is not interested in moving others to action because she does not see herself as important enough to change the actions of others. Her attention, therefore, is turned inward, to analyzing and controlling through art her complex mental landscape. She is obsessed with the concept of gender, which to her is just another of many divisive factors contributing to her isolation.

In respect to the attitude toward gender, there is a fundamental difference between *The Awakening* and *The Bell Jar*. Although Plath's and Chopin's works portray the same result, suicide, Chopin does not reject the female body and its functions as something evil. Rather she rejects society's mirror image of that body and the distortions it imposes on women's psyches. Chopin externalizes the causes of woman's plight, while Plath internalizes them, developing a self-loathing which is a fundamental cause of suicide. In this respect, Gilbert and Gubar's insights into the causes of women's suicides discussed in the first chapter are more applicable to Plath than to Chopin. Just because Plath embraced the domestic myth of the angel in the house, she is not any less the victim of this dichotomy. Edna Pontellier may have consciously understood the reason why suicide was the only choice left to her; Esther's knowledge is instinctive.

To further bolster his arguments against a feminist approach to Plath's work, Rosenblatt states, "Plath's attitude toward men and women is never stated in an ideological fashion in her prose; and the various contradictory perceptions of male and female situations in the poems suggest that she possessed no consistent viewpoint on this issue" (9). Plath's agony was personal, not ideological, and while she felt her femininity intensely, she was suspicious of all relationships, whether with men or women. Plath could be characterized as the ambivalent observer of the world around her, and that is how she portrays her protagonist Esther Greenwood in *The Bell Jar*. Esther says,

> I liked looking on at other people in crucial situations. If there was a road accident or a street fight or a baby pickled in a laboratory jar for me to look at, I'd stop and look so hard I never forgot it.
>
> I certainly learned a lot of things I never would have learned otherwise this way, and even when they surprised me or made me sick I never let on, but pretended that's the way I knew things were all the time. (14)

Esther spends much of her time in New York observing the various lifestyles of the women characters around her trying to decide what she wants to be herself. Esther is at the crucial point in her life when she must make decisions concerning her adult identity. She recognizes the discrepancy between the world of school and of work; however, she cannot see the bridge between her present existence and the future. Esther states,

> The one thing I was good at was winning scholarships and prizes, and that era was coming to an end.
>
> I felt like a racehorse in a world without racetracks or a champion college

footballer suddenly confronted by Wall Street and a business suit, his days of glory shrunk to a little gold cup on his mantel with a date engraved on it like the date on a tombstone. (84)

Later in the novel, as her identity deteriorates, she thinks,

I saw the years of my life spaced along a road in the form of telephone poles, threaded together by wires. I counted one, two, three…nineteen telephones poles, and then the wires dangled into space, and try as I would, I couldn't see a single pole beyond the nineteenth. (137)

In Chapter I, the retrospective longing for childhood by female characters was noted by Nina Auerbach. Esther too longs for this childhood saying, "I was only purely happy until I was nine years old" (82), the year of her father's death. At the age of nineteen, Esther realizes that her childhood is no longer within her reach, although she attempts symbolically to regress back to it throughout the novel. Her longings are prompted by the fact that she sees no experience as an adult that will compensate her for that loss.

When Esther arrives in New York, she looks for role models to emulate. First, she is taken with the sexpot Doreen, who is one of the twelve guest editors that summer. Esther says,

I'd never known a girl like Doreen before. Doreen came from a society girl's college down South and had bright white hair standing out in a cotton candy fluff round her head and blue eyes like transparent agate marbles, hard and polished and just about indestructible, and a mouth set in a sort of perpetual sneer. I don't mean a nasty sneer, but an amused mysterious sneer, as if all the people around her were pretty silly and she could tell some good jokes on them if she wanted to. (5)

It is not hard to recognize in Doreen the Fair Goddess as bitch of Leslie Fiedler or the monster of Gilbert and Gubar, and just as Edna Pontellier is attracted to various female characters as prototypes in *The Awakening*, Esther is attracted to Doreen. Esther notes, "Everything she said was like a secret voice speaking straight out of my own bones" (8). However, this involvement is rather brief. Esther abandons her friend one night when Doreen arrives back at their hotel in a drunken stupor:

I made a decision about Doreen that night. I decided I would watch her and listen to what she said, but deep down I would have nothing at all to do with her. Deep down, I would be loyal to Betsy and her innocent friends. It was Betsy I resembled at heart. (25)

Esther describes Doreen's opposite, the angel Betsy, as being "imported...straight from Kansas with her bouncing blonde ponytail and Sweetheart-of-Sigma-Chi smile" (7). According to Esther, "Betsy was always asking me to do things with her and the other girls as if she were trying to save me in some way" (7), which she was. But, of course, Esther bears no resemblance to the cow-like Betsy despite her efforts to convince herself otherwise, nor does she truly want to. Rather Esther feels that she ought to want to be like Betsy, and she cannot quite give up society's flawed concept of women as being either angels or monsters.

Although Esther attempts for a short time to embrace the lifestyle represented by Betsy, she is symbolically rejected as not being suitable for that kind of pure but bovine existence. Immediately after the scene in the novel where she resolves to have nothing more to do with Doreen, Esther attends a lavish luncheon at the "hygienic white" Food Testing Kitchens at *Ladies' Day* with Betsy and the other girls (27). However, the hypocrisy of the domestic myth put forth by *Ladies' Day*, which Esther already suspects, is symbolically revealed when all of the girls including Esther get desperately ill with ptomaine poisoning from the food. Esther has "a vision of the celestially white kitchens of *Ladies' Day* stretching into infinity" and the food it produces is "poison" (52). Gladys Milliner in "The Tragic Imperative: *The Awakening* and *The Bell Jar*" rightly concludes that the stomach of the poisoned Esther "literally reject[s] the false image of the pure American woman represented by *Ladies' Day*" (22). Ironically, it is Doreen, the only one who did not attend the luncheon and therefore did not get ill, who nurses Esther back to health.

Esther's other role model is Jay Cee, the career woman who is an editor at *Ladies' Day*. Esther describes her as follows:

> Jay Cee was my boss, and I liked her a lot, in spite of what Doreen said. She wasn't one of the fashion magazine gushers with fake eyelashes and giddy jewelry. Jay Cee had brains, so her plug-ugly looks didn't seem to matter. She read a couple of languages and knew all the quality writers in the business. (6)

Jay Cee seems fond of Esther and wants to help her; however, Esther states that all the old women "wanted to adopt me in some way, and, for the price of their care and influence, have me resemble them" (248), a prospect which she resists. Jay Cee stands as a parallel to Mademoiselle Reisz of *The Awakening*. Both women have embraced the life of significant action as artist but at the cost of sacrificing their sexuality in the process. As Edna rejects the roles of earth mother and artist, Esther rejects the models of sexpot and career woman.

However, this rejection of stereotypical roles does not provide Esther with a sense of identity, merely an awareness of the limitations that these roles all entail. In a key image in the novel Esther says:

> I saw my life branching out before me like the green fig tree in the story.
>
>   From the tip of every branch, like a fat purple fig, a wonderful future beckoned and winked. One fig was a husband and a happy home and children, and another fig was a famous poet and another fig was a brilliant professor, and another fig was Ee Gee, the amazing editor, and another fig was Europe and Africa and South America, and another fig was Constantin and Socrates and Attila and a pack of other lovers with queer names and offbeat professions, and another fig was an Olympic lady crew champion, and beyond and above these figs were many more figs I couldn't quite make out.
>
>   I saw myself sitting in the crotch of this fig tree, starving to death, just because I couldn't make up my mind which of the figs I would choose. I wanted each and every one of them, but choosing one meant losing all the rest, and, as I sat there, unable to decide, the figs began to wrinkle and go black, and, one by one, they plopped to the ground at my feet. (84-5)

It is interesting to note how similar in this respect Edna Pontellier and Esther are. Both feel ambivalent about the choices open to them. They feel that any choice is too limiting for women because too little of their lives can be integrated into only one of these choices; too much of significance must be left out. In the midst of the feast of life, Esther is starving because each experience is only temporarily satisfying. Both Esther and Edna may not be starving for food like some anorexic nineteenth-century heroines, but they are starved for life.

In response, both Edna and Esther allow themselves to be carried along passively by their impulses rather than make such unacceptable and limiting choices. While in New York, Esther identifies this conflict and the resulting apathy:

> I told Doreen I would not go to the show or the luncheon or the film premiere, but that I would not go to Coney Island either, I would stay in bed. After Doreen left, I wondered why I couldn't go the whole way doing what I should anymore. This made me sad and tired. Then I wondered why I couldn't go the whole way doing what I shouldn't, the way Doreen did, and this made me even sadder and more tired. (32)

Esther's inability to make a choice is fueling her depression and anger. Linda Wagner-Martin concludes in *Sylvia Plath: A Biography* that Plath's use of irony in the novel implies "that a woman does not have to make that single choice. Her dilemma is entirely artificial. Only social pressure forces the choice" (186). But Esther cannot see past the social constructs. When Plath writes the novel, a decade after the events on which the novel is based occurred, she can present her earlier suffering in an objective, ironic light.

As the novel progresses, Esther retreats more and more to sleep and finally to suicide as a means of exerting some control over her circumstances. As Caroline King Barnard points out in *Sylvia Plath*:

> Esther is an unwilling captive of her background and conditioning; external, familial and social pressures war with her natural instincts, and her level of self-confidence is far too low for those instincts to assert themselves sufficiently. Her naive expectations of sex and marriage, for example, have been thoroughly conditioned by her mother and by others: to be acceptable as a wife she must remain a virgin, and after marriage she must assume a submissive domestic role. Instinctively she rebels against these notions, partly because she naturally senses their limitations, and partly because she discovers that men are not bound by similar premarital rules. The confusion thereby produced is extreme. (25–6)

As Barnard sees, men are not bound by the same arbitrary and artificial rules that women are. Esther's confusion is increased by her inability to completely accept or reject this dichotomy. Her ambivalence becomes the driving force behind her breakdown. Ultimately, some compromises have to be made by Esther in order for her to forge a new identity that will signal the beginning of her recovery.

Esther's breakdown, which had barely begun in New York, develops swiftly when she returns to her home. Esther notes, "I had never spent a summer in the suburbs before" (128), and "I made a point of never living in the same house with my mother for more than a week" (132). Esther's mother is one of those women who sacrifice everything for their children and in return expect their children to perfectly fulfill their fantasies for them. Of course, this expectation puts tremendous pressure on the child to perform. In an effort to mollify her mother, Plath sometimes maintained that Mrs. Greenwood was not patterned on Mrs. Plath, but it is clear that, as with the rest of Plath's work, the characterization here is highly autobiographical. For example, a real life parallel occurred when Plath suffered her final breakdown; she begged her brother to keep her mother from coming to see her, knowing that she would merely have to expend additional energy putting up a front for her. The underlying hatred that Plath felt for her mother becomes evident in Esther's reaction also. As *The Bell Jar* develops, it becomes clear that her mother's unrealistic expectations for Esther are contributing to Esther's breakdown.

Mrs. Greenwood is never able to see Esther as a separate individual with her own needs and wants. When Esther rebels against the shock treatments prescribed by her doctor saying that she is not coming back for further treatment, the following conversation ensues:

> Her mother smiled. "I knew my baby wasn't like that."
> I looked at her. "Like what?"
> "Like those awful people. Those awful dead people at that hospital." She paused, "I knew you'd decide to be all right again." (163)

Esther's mother refuses to see how sick and out of control Esther is.

After her subsequent suicide attempt when Esther is institutionalized, she dreads visits from her mother:

> My mother was the worst. She never scolded me, but kept begging me, with a sorrowful face, to tell her what she had done wrong. She said she was sure the doctors thought she had done something wrong because they asked her a lot of questions about my toilet training, and I had been perfectly trained at a very early age and given her no trouble whatsoever. (228)

The major breakthrough that contributes to her recovery comes when Esther admits her true feelings for her mother to Dr. Nolan:

> "I hate her," I said, and waited for the blow to fall.
> But Dr. Nolan only smiled at me as if something had pleased her very, very much, and said, "I suppose you do." (229)

Mrs. Greenwood represents the mythic all-consuming mother, but there are other negative maternal images in the novel as well.

Esther feels that fundamentally her identity as a person exists only in opposition to the stereotypical roles of the suburban housewife and mother. In the suburbs as on Grand Isle, there are the mother-women. In *The Bell Jar*, the mother-woman is Dodo Conway. Esther describes her totally in negative terms:

> A woman not five feet tall, with a grotesque, protruding stomach, was wheeling an old black baby carriage down the street. Two or three small children of various sizes, all pale, with smudgy faces and bare smudgy knees, wobbled along in the shadow of her skirts. (129)

Dodo has six children and is about to have her seventh, all of them subsisting "on Rice Krispies, peanut-butter-and-marshmallow sandwiches, vanilla ice cream and gallon upon gallon of Hoods milk" (130). Milliner describes Dodo as "the modern suburban housewife...typical of the woman who has had a superior education, only to become a housewife and mother" (24). Picturing herself in that role, Esther thinks,

> This seemed a dreary and wasted life for a girl with fifteen years of straight A's, but I knew that's what marriage was like...I knew in spite of all the roses and kisses and restaurant dinners a man showered on a woman before he married her, what he secretly wanted when the wedding service ended was for her to flatten out underneath his feet like Mrs. Willard's kitchen mat. (93–4)

Esther realizes that she cannot stay in the suburbs with the mother-women, but she has lost the will to escape because she has no vision of a place to escape to.

Ultimately, she is immobilized by her lack of personal identity. As Barnard points out, Esther has derived her identity from others, trying to live up to the expectations of those around her (26). Now, whenever she tries to take any of these actions, her body rebels on her, refusing to cooperate. "My hand advanced a few inches, then retreated and fell limp. I forced it toward the receiver again, but again it stopped short, as if it had collided with a pane of glass" (132). The bell jar had descended.

To cure Esther of her depression, her family sends her to see the male psychiatrist, Dr. Gordon, who is portrayed as smug and conceited. Esther realizes immediately that the doctor who is supposed to help her could have no way of understanding the conflicts that she feels: "I thought, how could this Doctor Gordon help me anyway, with a beautiful wife and beautiful children and a beautiful dog haloing him like the angels on a Christmas card?" (145). Dr. Gordon is just another example of Esther's estrangement from patriarchical society. He doesn't want to understand her—he barely even speaks to her and then only about his experiences at her college in his youth—rather, he wants to fix her like a broken machine, so his immediate response is to prescribe shock treatments. The novel begins with Esther's preoccupation with the impending electrocution of the Rosenbergs: "I couldn't help wondering what it would be like, being burned alive all along your nerves" (1). She gets her answer at Dr. Gordon's private hospital:

> Then something bent down and took hold of me and shook me like the end of the world. Whee-ee-ee-ee-ee, it shrilled, through an air crackling with blue light, and with each flash a great bolt drubbed me till I thought my bones would break and

the sap fly out of me like a split plant.
I wondered what terrible thing it was that I had done. (161)

What Esther had done was to be born a woman. She realizes immediately that Dr. Gordon's method of treatment is not going to help her, and she resolves not to continue seeing him. Instead, she develops her own solution to her problems—suicide.

Esther's approach to suicide is methodical rather than impulsive like Edna's. She explores several possible ways of committing suicide—using razor blades or a gun, or even drowning. She describes her attempts to drown:

I brought my hands to my breast, ducked my head, and dived, using my hands to push the water aside. The water pressed in on my eardrums and on my heart. I fanned myself down, but before I knew where I was, the water had spat me up into the sun, the world was sparkling all about me like blue and green and yellow semi-precious stones. (181)

Milliner says, "Esther Greenwood, like Edna, tries to end her life in the sea, but it is impossible to do so because for her the sea is a symbol of life" (25). Esther's happiest memories are of the time she spent with her father at the seashore. She is unable to make the sea into an instrument of her death. Freud, interpreting suicide methods symbolically, says that "to drown is to bear a child" (qtd. in Higonnet 69), but Esther does not wish to bear a child; she wishes to become one, even to regress back to the womb herself. Barnard states that the act of suicide represents for Esther "a total withdrawal to the 'pure' and 'sweet' condition of infancy" (29).

At several points in the novel, Esther reveals her obsession with purity that she associates with a baby. Early in the novel, after her disillusioning escapade with Doreen in New York, she ritually cleanses herself in a bath.

I said to myself: "Doreen is dissolving, Lenny Shepherd is dissolving, Frankie is dissolving, New York is dissolving, they are all dissolving away and none of them matter any more. I don't know them, I have never known them and I am very pure. All that liquor and those sticky kisses I say and the dirt that settled on my skin on the way back is turning into something pure."
    The longer I lay there in the clear hot water the purer I felt, and when I stepped out at last and wrapped myself in one of the big, soft white hotel bath towels I felt pure and sweet as a new baby. (22)

Mason Harris in his review of the novel notes the relationship between Esther's longing for regression to a state of infancy and her feelings of stifled personal development symbolized by the use of baby-images:

> Pleasant baby-images are associated with the joys of regression but the novel is
> also haunted by the nightmare image of a fetus in a bottle...This aspect of the baby
> becomes a graphic expression of that sense of strangled development which is the
> other side of her tendency to regression. (36)

In addition to longing for the innocence and promise of childhood, Plath presents the flip side of Nina Auerbach's dream of the intact child. In Plath's negative vision, the child merely becomes pickled in its own juices in a bottle, its existence circular and sterile.

Esther's final solution to her confusion is to take fifty sleeping pills and to crawl down into a secluded portion of the basement to die. To ensure that she will not be searched for and found too soon, she leaves a note saying that she has gone for a long walk. Only by the sheerest luck does Esther survive this attempt and begin her recovery that involves building a new identity for herself. Barnard concludes that from her experience of suicide, "Esther does achieve a sort of rebirth, though perhaps not precisely the variety she had expected. Her suicide attempt fails, and she is hospitalized. Yet, in her total collapse, she has reached a kind of infancy, from which she can grow" (30). In the institution, Esther begins to pull together the fragments of her personality.

As has been noted, several parallels clearly exist between *The Awakening* and *The Bell Jar*. Both center on the search for identity by the female protagonist, a process, which involves her observation and investigation of the various traditional female roles. These parallels do not exist because Plath was purposely building on the work of Chopin; there is no evidence that Plath was even aware of Chopin's work. The parallels exist because Plath and Chopin are dealing with the same subject, a subject that Susan Rosowski delineates in "The Novel of Awakening." Rosowski notes the similarity between this theme in novels by women with the *bildungsroman* or apprenticeship novel that has appeared in literature by men:

> The novel of awakening is similar to the apprenticeship novel in some ways: it also
> recounts the attempts of a sensitive protagonist to learn the nature of the world,
> discover its meaning and pattern, and acquire a philosophy of life, but she must
> learn these lessons in terms of herself as a woman. (43)

In the 1950s, as in the 1890s, the woman who strives for self-actualization has a quite different journey than a man who strives for the same goal. The novel of awareness is a good term to categorize *The Awakening* and *The Bell Jar*, for as Rosowski states:

> The subject and action of the novel of awakening characteristically consist of a protagonist who attempts to find value in a world defined by love and marriage. The direction of awakening follows what is becoming a pattern in literature by and about women; movement is inward toward greater self knowledge that leads in turn to a revelation of the disparity between that self knowledge and the nature of the world. The protagonist's growth results typically not with "an art of living," as for her male counterpart, but instead with the realization that for a woman, such an art of living is difficult or impossible; it is an awakening to limitations. (43)

Esther's nervous breakdown and suicide attempt are her rebellion against these limitations. Her resulting psychiatric therapy is the process by which she attempts to develop skills to cope with these limitations. However, to Mary Ellmann, "It is apparent that if such events constitute reality, madness is as plausible as sanity....The novel scarcely indicates what there is to be sane *for*, beyond escaping the fustiness of insanity" (225). In this respect, the conclusions of *The Bell Jar* and *The Awakening* are similar. Esther's apparent cure is only a postponement of the inevitable. One would predict that Esther would follow Edna's course when she too reaches the age of twenty-nine, after experiencing marriage, motherhood, and passion and finding them insufficient. The convergence of fiction and biography is that exactly describes what happened to Plath.

Another parallel that exists between *The Awakening* and *The Bell Jar* is in their authors' use of the male characters as agents of limitation and oppression. The primary male agent in *The Bell Jar* is Esther's boyfriend and almost fiance, Buddy Willard. Milliner writes that in the relationship between Esther and Buddy, "Sylvia Plath explores the problem of the superior woman who must suppress her own capabilities in order to please a man" (23). Before she and Buddy began dating, Esther had mooned after him for five years, thinking "he was the most wonderful boy I'd ever seen" (57). However, Esther soon learns that he is a "hypocrite" when she finds out that he has gone to bed with another girl (57). Esther is shocked; "I never thought for one minute that Buddy Willard would have an affair with anyone. I expected him to say, 'No, I have been saving myself for when I get married to someone pure and a virgin like you'" (76). On the other hand, Esther feels that society is trying to restrict her choices by continually pressuring her to remain pure:

> ...the best men wanted to be pure for their wives, and even if they weren't pure,

they wanted to be the ones to teach their wives about sex. Of course, they would try to persuade a girl to have sex, and say they would marry her later, but as soon as she gave in, they would lose all respect for her and start saying that if she did that with them she would do that with other men and they would end up by making her life miserable. (89)

Esther resists this double standard that she feels victimizes women.

Esther encounters two other male figures in the novel who overtly reinforce the concept that to be loved, a woman must be pure. She has a brief conversation with a boy named Eric who tells her sex is boring. The following dialogue ensues:

I said maybe if you loved a woman it wouldn't seem so boring, but Eric said it would be spoiled by thinking this woman too was just an animal like the rest, so if he loved anybody he would never go to bed with her. He'd go to a whore if he had to and keep the woman he loved free of all that dirty business. (87)

Esther has a more violent and traumatic encounter with Marcos, her blind date at a party while she is still in New York. Marcos's only love is his cousin who is becoming a nun. Obviously, by loving her Marcos has set up a fable to protect himself from commitment to a real woman. To Marcos, all other women are "sluts." Five minutes into their date, he simply throws Esther down on the ground and attempts to rape her. Although Esther fights off his advances, she nevertheless internalizes the limited visions reflected by these male characters that reduce women to projections of masculine sexual experiences.

Not only is her boyfriend Buddy a hypocrite about sex, but throughout the novel he constantly attempts to undermine Esther's identity as a writer and an independent human being. Buddy makes fun of Esther's work, calling a poem "just a piece of dust" (62). Since Buddy is in medical school, at her request, he takes Esther to see a woman giving birth. In a speech that closely parallels Dr. Mandelet's in *The Awakening*, a friend of Buddy's tells Esther, "You oughtn't to see this…You'll never want to have a baby if you do. They oughtn't to let women watch. It'll be the end of the human race" (71). It is just after this scene that Buddy, pushing Esther towards having sex with him, undresses to offer her the "educational" opportunity to see a man naked. Unfortunately, what Esther sees reminds her primarily of "turkey neck and turkey gizzards" (75). In his efforts to dominate and indoctrinate Esther, Buddy cites his mother as a paragon of what a wife and mother should be: "He was always saying how his mother said, 'What a man wants is a mate and what a woman wants is infinite security,' and 'What a man is is an arrow into the future and what a woman is is the place the arrow shoots off from'" (79). In an effort to further undermine Esther's confidence in her own judgment, Buddy implies that a normal woman would not be interested in being a writer. Esther says, "I also remembered Buddy Willard saying in a sinister, knowing way that after I had children I would feel differently, I wouldn't want to write poems any more" (94). Esther's response to this is to think, "…maybe it was true that when you were married and had children it was like being brainwashed, and afterward you went about numb as a slave in some private, totalitarian state"(94), hardly an attractive image for marriage and motherhood. It is no wonder that Esther comes to the conclusion that for a woman with ambition and intelligence, marriage and children must be avoided at all costs.

Thus Esther, attempting to determine her identity on the verge of becoming a woman, rebels against the sexual double standard that she sees is at the center of the patriarchical institution of marriage, stating, "I couldn't stand the idea of a woman having to have a single pure life and a man being able to have a double life, one pure and one not" (90-1). Like Anna Karenina, Emma Bovary, and Edna Pontellier before her, Esther (much more naively) acts out her rebellion by actively seeking illicit sex. Milliner points out that Esther "deliberately and dispassionately sets out to equalize the double standard in sexual relations" (24) by seducing some man, preferably a total stranger.

As we have seen, the sex act is often fraught with negative consequences for women, but Esther is freed from the most significant consequence of sex, an unwanted pregnancy, by the last female role model in the novel, Dr. Nolan, the woman psychiatrist who helps Esther lift the bell jar and who also serves as a positive maternal figure, providing Esther with one of the few integrated female role models in the novel. When Esther confesses that she "hates the thought of being under a man's thumb" because "A man doesn't have a worry in the world, while I've got a baby hanging over my head like a big stick, to keep me in line" (249), Dr. Nolan prescribes a diaphragm as a means of birth control for Esther, thereby giving her a sense of personal control and thus freedom. Soon afterwards, Esther loses her virginity, but she ironically ends up in the emergency room of the hospital due to excessive hemorrhaging from her first sexual experience. Milliner writes, "In a sense, even though she initiated the experience, Esther is a symbolical sacrificial victim of man" (24). Even in situations where Esther has planned carefully to maintain personal control, this control eludes her. In literature by women about women, this is a repeated theme. The theories and rules that seemingly work for men in controlling their experiences do not work for women, and, in fact, often work against them.

The diaphragm that Dr. Nolan provides is just one symbol of Esther's increased self-confidence that is the foundation for her new, more integrated personality. Caroline King Barnard notes the most important landmark in Esther's journey to recovery:

> Esther achieves sufficient perspective to see that her struggle against the tyranny of custom and expectation is not hers alone, but is generally characteristic of the human condition. Her hospital environment is little different from the college environment which she has left and to which she will return. (31)

Because of the suicide of her psychic double, Joan Gilling, Esther also, at least temporarily, rids herself of the need to commit suicide. Several critical analyses have focused on the use of the double in *The Bell Jar*, most notably Vance Bourjaily's "Victoria Lucas and Elly Higginbottom" and Gordon Lameyer's "The Double in Sylvia Plath's *The Bell Jar*." Lameyer points out that Plath's honor's thesis at Smith was a study of the double in two of Fyodor Dostoevsky's novels. In *The Bell Jar*, Plath's alter-ego, Esther, is working on an honor's thesis on the double in Joyce's *Finnegans Wake*. Obviously, Plath uses the concept of the double as a motif in her novel, and the novel abounds with these images.

According to Lameyer, the most important double that appears in the second half of the book is Joan Gilling, whose death as Esther's surrogate allows Esther to complete the healing process. Bourjaily echoes Lameyer in stating, "Others have seen *The Bell Jar* as a book full of Esther-doubles, but in my reading only Joan is truly one" (139). We first meet Joan early in the novel as one of Esther's classmates and Buddy Willard's former girlfriend. Esther states,

> Joan Gilling came from our hometown and went to our church and was a year ahead of me in college. She was a big wheel—president of her class and a physics major and the college hockey champion. She always made me feel squirmy with her starey pebble-colored eyes and her gleaming tombstone teeth and her breathy voice. (65)

When Esther moves to McLean, her last sanitarium, she is surprised to find that Joan is in the adjoining room that "was a mirror image of my own" (220). Joan, following Esther's example—she had read about her in the paper—had also tried to kill herself, and Esther realizes, "For the first time it occurred to me that Joan and I might have something in common" (225). Later Esther says of the relationship with Joan which develops in the sanitarium, "It was as if we had been forced together by some overwhelming circumstance, like war or plague, and shared a world of our own" (253).

Even though she and Joan have shared experiences, Esther is still ambivalent in her feelings towards others. When Joan is found to be missing from the sanitarium, Esther says, "Suddenly, I wanted to disassociate myself from Joan completely" (264), her exact reaction to an earlier double figure, Doreen. This rejection stems from Esther's need to project her negative nature onto those around her and then reject them in the hopes of purifying herself. It is Joan who ultimately succeeds in the game of suicide, hanging herself in the woods outside the sanitarium one freezing winter's night. When Esther attends Joan's funeral, she wonders "what I thought I was burying" (273), but at least temporarily, Esther appears to be burying her need for self-punishment and personal annihilation. Concerning the function of the double the novel, Lameyer concludes:

> The early material about Joan Gilling is strictly biographical. The original was a girl named Jane whom Sylvia really admired. But here is one place where Sylvia materially altered her experience for the sake of the novel's structure. As the heroine's main double in McLean, Joan had to die, allowing the good side of the heroine to emerge cured. (159)

As she leaves the sanitarium at the conclusion of the novel, Esther describes herself in a curiously mixed metaphor, as "being born twice— patched, retreaded and approved for the road" (275). However, Mason Harris in his review of *The Bell Jar* states,

> In the end Esther's cure seems to consist more of resignation to prison than escape from it. If madness was precipitated by a demand for something better than the compulsive past, recovered sanity seems a depressing return to her "old best self" because nothing better has been found. (38)

Although Esther is momentarily in control, the reader is left wondering like Esther if "someday—at college, in Europe, somewhere, anywhere—the bell jar, with its stifling distortions, wouldn't descend again?" (271).

Although the events related in *The Bell Jar* took place in the summer of 1953, Plath substantially wrote the novel in 1962, and it was published in England in January 1963 under the assumed name of Victoria Lucas.

Reviewer Geoffrey Wolff notes, "The novel has a special poignancy, of course, because it shuts down on the upbeat note of cure, and we know the end of the author's life" (113). Shortly after the publication of *The Bell Jar*, on the morning of February 11, 1963, Plath killed herself. A. Alvarez notes that her first suicide attempt, chronicled in the novel, was methodically thought out and carefully executed and should have succeeded, but, ironically, it failed. Her final attempt seemed planned for failure but ironically succeeded (she left a note for her *au pair* girl to call her doctor, but she wasn't discovered in time). As Alvarez says, "She gambled for the last time, having worked out that the odds were in her favor, but perhaps, in her depression, not much caring whether she won or lost. Her calculations went wrong and she lost" (39-40).

In the biographical notes to the 1981 edition of the novel, Lois Ames asks, "Who can explain *why*?" (216). The common explanation for Plath's suicide is that after a year of illness coupled with the discovery of infidelity on the part of her husband and the stress of caring for two small children, the bell jar once again descended for Plath. Milliner, the only critic to compare Chopin and Plath, states,

> In the suicide of Edna and the attempted suicide of Esther, in the death of Kate Chopin as an artist and the death of the artist Sylvia Plath, there are the elements of the universal tragedy of women frustrated in their efforts to fulfill themselves as human beings. In their own lives and art and in the aspirations and disappointments of their protagonists, Chopin and Plath have exemplified the tragedy of women awakened to their human potential, only to discover that they have awakened to a nightmare because that potential can never be fully realized. (26)

Esther herself observes, "To the person in the bell jar, blank and stopped as a dead baby, the world itself is the bad dream" (267). Plath explores this nightmare world even more fully in her poetry.

CHAPTER IV

Ariel, Plath on the Edge

The Bell Jar ends with Esther's presumed release from the sanitarium and her return mid-year to college. Plath portrays this event as an act of rebirth, stating in the closing sentence, "The eyes and the faces all turned themselves toward me, and guiding myself by them, as by a magical thread, I stepped into the room" (275). In real life, too, Plath returned to Smith College to resume her studies, and in June 1955 she graduated summa cum laude. Soon after graduation, Plath, having received a Fulbright fellowship to Cambridge University, departed for England. While at Cambridge, in March 1956, she met the future poet laureate, Ted Hughes, and they married in June of that year. For a period of time, Plath seemed to have attained her vision of the perfect family. Both the poets continued to be published and recognized for their work, and they had two children, Freda and Nicholas, recreating substantially the structure of Plath's own family as she was growing up. In 1961 they bought an old manor house in Devon. As Caroline King Barnard concludes, "For a time, life in their new country home proved fruitful and rewarding. The Hugheses established a writing schedule, enabling Sylvia to write in the morning while Ted wrote in the afternoon" (22).

However, before long, cracks began to show in the facade of Plath's family life. Hughes was absent from Devon frequently, ostensibly for business reasons. But as Plath subsequently discovered, he was actually having an affair with a family friend, Assia Wevill. For several months, Plath continued to live with Hughes, hoping the marriage could be salvaged; however, in December 1962, she and the children moved to an apartment in London, where she subsequently killed herself in February 1963. In this final year that saw the shattering of her family, Plath wrote most of the poems that appear in *Ariel.*

During this period of intense writing, Plath had projected publishing a volume of poetry, which went through various name changes, depending on the most recent poem she had written, before she finally decided on *Ariel.* Linda Wagner-Martin in her biography of Plath elaborates on the title choice:

> It was only with "Ariel," God's lioness, that she chose a rich enough image to free the reader's imagination: androgynous power, animal made human and spirit, the whimsicality of Shakespeare's character in *The Tempest.* Sylvia chose a title that

stressed her affinity with a liberating imagination and thereby drew a portrait of the
woman as artist. The magic of Plath's collection occurs because domestic events
are transformed by art. Sylvia, too, was an Ariel, using "art to enchant" and earning
her freedom through truthfulness. (226–27)

The collection of poems entitled *Ariel* was first published in 1965 in England,
two years after Plath's death. The American edition came out the next year
with an introduction by Robert Lowell, who describes the Plath who produced
this poetry as "hardly a person at all, or a woman, certainly not another
'poetess'" (vii), a typically male tribute that ostensibly praises Plath for
writing like a man.

The voice in *Ariel* was soon seen as unique. In *Stealing the Language:
The Emergence of Women's Poetry in America*, Alicia Ostriker states,
"*Ariel*...gave many readers their first taste of unapologetic anger in a
woman's poems" (78). Katha Pollitt says in her review of Plath's poetry,
"...by the time she came to write her last seventy or eighty poems, there was
no other voice like hers on earth" (qtd. in Wagner 1). Elizabeth Hardwick
notes the source of this voice stating, "Perhaps it is important to remember
that the poems are about suicide rather than about death as the waiting
denouement of every life" (107). She adds, "Suicides are frequent enough, but
the love of death, the teasing joy of it are rarely felt" (105).

The source of Plath's suicidal impulses is her need to achieve perfection,
which she identifies with the concept of purity, even of virginity. As has
already been seen in the analysis of *The Bell Jar*, purity has a redemptive and
transcendent power for Plath. There her protagonist Esther Greenwood states,

When I was nineteen, pureness was the great issue.

   Instead of the world being divided up into Catholics and Protestants or
Republicans and Democrats or white men and black men or even men and women,
I saw the world divided into people who had slept with somebody and people who
hadn't, and this seemed the only really significant difference between one person
and another. (90)

Superficially, Plath seems to be mirroring the moral platitudes of America in
the 1950s that saw women's bodies as the battleground for the evil in the
world. Certainly, in *The Bell Jar* the adolescent sexual context for purity
seems a relatively normal focus of interest and concern for the nineteen-year-
old female protagonist. However, Plath's violent obsession with the subject in
her work foreshadows her own tragic end. According to the sociologist Ronald
Maris, "It seems likely that what psychiatrist Robert Litman calls 'ego–

splitting' was a fundamental by-product of Sylvia's relationship with her father. Litman contends that ego-splitting occurs when a hated external object is internalized...then that death wish for the hated external object is turned back upon the ego" (129). Such a concept seems to be at work in *The Bell Jar*. When Esther is exploring her various options for suicide, she contemplates slashing her wrists with razor blades, but she rejects that option, stating,

> But when it came right down to it, the skin of my wrist looked so white and defenseless that I couldn't do it. It was as if what I wanted to kill wasn't in that skin or the thin blue pulse that jumped under my thumb, but somewhere else, deeper, more secret, a whole lot harder to get at. (165)

In the context of the novel, that deep inner spirit tormenting Esther is connected to the loss of her father. Immediately prior to her suicide attempt, Esther visits her father's grave. She says,

> I thought it odd that in all the time my father had been buried in this graveyard, none of us had ever visited him. My mother hadn't let us come to his funeral because we were only children then, and he had died in the hospital, so the graveyard and even his death had always seemed unreal to me. (186)

Esther decides that as the oldest and her "father's favorite" she should "take on a mourning my mother had never bothered with" (186). When she finds her father's grave, she is surprised by the intensity of her emotions:

> My legs folded under me, and I sat down in the sopping grass. I couldn't understand why I was crying so hard.
>
> Then I remembered that I had never cried for my father's death.
>
> My mother hadn't cried either. She had just smiled and said what a merciful thing it was for him he had died, because if he had lived he would have been crippled and an invalid for life, and he couldn't have stood that, he would rather have died than had that happen.
>
> I laid my face to the smooth face of the marble and howled my loss into the cold salt rain. (188–9)

What Esther hints at here, she states elsewhere in the book; her mother is actually glad that the father has died. The father is portrayed as aloof and dictatorial, so the daughter has absorbed both the child's love and need for the father and the mother's relief that he is gone. These attitudes introduced in *The Bell Jar*, which was written concurrently with *Ariel*, are reflected even

more strongly in Plath's poems in that volume which deal specifically with
suicide, "Daddy," "Lady Lazarus," "Death & Co.," and "Edge."

In *The Awakening*, Kate Chopin presents her male characters
sympathetically. They are just as much products of their environment as the
women, and often just as confused and mystified by the conditions of life.
Although Leonce and Robert and even Alcee Arobin, the rake, are clearly
limited individuals, they are not evil, and Chopin does not portray them as
such. In *The Bell Jar*, the male characters are also generally portrayed as
limited in their awareness. Sometimes they are buffoons, but they are not
portrayed as singularly evil in their intent. However, in *Ariel* and particularly
in the poems "Lady Lazarus" and "Daddy," men are the source of evil and
oppression for the speaker in the poems.

"Daddy" is probably "the most anthologized of all Plath's poems"
(Blessing 66), perhaps because "Daddy" is one of the most accessible poems
in *Ariel* in its imagery and theme. "Daddy" is an angry outpouring of grief by
an adult daughter who feels abandoned and betrayed by her father's death
when she was a child. She has found this early experience to be a pattern for
her relationships with all men, and the poem is a denouncement of men's
relationships with women. Plath couches her sense of the male-female
relationship in contemporary cultural images of oppression and exploitation.
A consistent metaphor that appears in Plath's late poems is her identification
with the Jewish experience during World War II. Plath herself summarized the
content of "Daddy" in an interview, saying:

> The poem is spoken by a girl with an Electra complex. Her father died while she
> thought he was God. Her case is complicated by the fact that her father was also a
> Nazi and her mother very possibly part Jewish. In the daughter the two strains
> marry and paralyze each other.
> She has to act out the awful little allegory once over before she is free of it.
> (qtd. in Kenner 34)

But Hugh Kenner concludes that Plath is playing a game with her audience, if
not herself, with this glib explanation. He sees Plath as hiding behind a series
of masks, her public rationales for her poetry just that (34).

While Kenner doubts that artistic distance exists as Plath claims in
"Daddy," critics such as Richard Allan Blessing and Harold Bloom object
strongly to Plath's use of the Jewish experience as a metaphor in her poetry.
Bloom states in his introduction to *Sylvia Plath: Modern Critical Views* that
the "gratuitous and humanly offensive appropriation of the imagery of Jewish
martyrs in Nazi death camps (an appropriation incessant in Plath) seems to

me a pure instance of coercive rhetoric, transforming absolutely nothing. That the reader is harangued, not persuaded, is my baffled protest" (3-4). Blessing, too, faults Plath for this appropriation in "Daddy" and other poems, arguing:

> Finally Plath is only the tiniest bit of a Jew and one feels that she claims too much for her suffering. Otto Plath and Ted Hughes are not Himmler and Hitler; her life is not a train ride to a concentration camp. One hears the sound of madness in this confession, the same self-pitying overreaction that one finds in the letters home about her chemistry difficulties or the suicide attempt triggered by a rejection from a summer writing program. Thus the poem travels from overstatement to overstatement and back. (67)

Although Bloom and Blessing are firm in their damnation of Plath for her use of Jewish imagery in her poetry, they do not attempt to analyze why this imagery appears in Plath's work; they are guilty of avoiding one of the basic questions of literary criticism—what was the writer's intent?

Actually, the reasons for Plath's identification with Jewish suffering are obvious and not particularly contrived or sinister. Plath, as we know, was a first generation American, an experience which brings with it its own identity problems. Her father was German, and to the child, Sylvia, he was an autocrat, who for most of her childhood was very ill. His sudden death when Plath was eight in 1940 was unexpected despite the seriousness of his illness. And apparently the way her mother chose to deal with this death created an air of mystery around it, which allowed Plath to further mythologize the events of her life. Of course, the major world events of this same period were dominated by Hitler and German aggression against other nations in Europe. Certainly, a sensitive and highly intelligent child and adolescent like Plath would feel the need to work out her relationship to the events in Europe that also seemed to be a metaphor for her own traumatic and difficult domestic life. Jewish suffering in the concentration camps was the overriding horror of the late 1940s of Plath's adolescence. Of the dichotomy of aggressor and victim, Plath naturally associated herself with the victim, as she consistently does with many politically-charged images. I refer here to her use of the Rosenbergs in *The Bell Jar* and her references to the Ku Klux Klan in the poem "Cut." Plath simply felt herself to be a victim of a world beyond her control, of a society that could not begin to understand the hundreds of slights and indignities that she had suffered primarily due to her gender. If a whole generation in the 1960s saw the Vietnam War as a symbol of oppression in its world, Plath in a like manner naturally saw the Jewish experience during World War II as a comparable symbol for hers.

This sense of victimization in "Daddy" is also reflected in another set of contemporary cultural images that Plath uses, drawn from the popular horror films of the 1930s and 1940s. This, too, Blessing finds offensive and superficial, describing the poem's concluding stanza where the villagers drive a stake through the vampire's heart as "the wonderful campy ending borrowed from a thousand late, late shows" (66). However, for the first time in her life, Plath was writing directly from her experience in the poems which appear in *Ariel* and *Winter Trees*. Plath's experience is the popular culture kitsch and the McCarthyism of the American 1950s: an era which exuberantly intended to put the war behind it by burying its ugliness in chrome and consumerism, a consumerism Plath ridicules in *The Bell Jar* when she has Esther say,

> I was supposed to be the envy of thousands of college girls just like me all over America who wanted nothing more than to be tripping about in those same size-seven patent leather shoes I'd bought at Bloomingdale's one lunch hour with a black patent leather belt and black patent leather pocketbook to match. (2)

Plath rebels against the America, which is intent on turning out robotic housewives to support an economic boom with the senseless buying of things neither wanted nor needed.

The Bell Jar also underscores Plath's anxiety over her German heritage. While Esther is a guest editor at *Ladies' Day* magazine, Jay Cee encourages her to learn German to elevate her above the other bright college girls competing for jobs in New York. But Esther states,

> I'd been telling people I'd always wanted to learn German for about five years.
> My mother spoke German during her childhood in America and was stoned for it during the First World War by the children at school. My German-speaking father, dead since I was nine, came from some manic-depressive hamlet in the black heart of Prussia.
> What I didn't say was that each time I picked up a German dictionary or a German book, the very sight of those dense, black, barbed-wire letters made my mind shut like a clam. (36)

These sentiments and conflicts that Plath sums up without rancor in *The Bell Jar* lie at the violent heart of "Daddy."

To understand "Daddy" the reader should start with Plath's "The Colossus," a poem "where the girl clambers in helpless self-absorption over the mammoth ruins of her father" (McClatchy 28). This effort effectively describes the lives of many wives, sisters, and daughters left with the legacy of sorting through and maintaining the mythos after the death of some male legend. Notable examples include Anna Freud, Mary Shelley, and Sophia Hawthorne. In Plath's case, it is not enough to reflect like a moon or a mirror someone else's life of significant action. In "Short Circuits and Folding Mirrors," J. D. McClatchy asserts that "The Colossus" is about remorse, but it is more about isolation and despair. The speaker addresses her father describing her lifetime of devoted care:

> Thirty years now I have laboured
> To dredge the silt from your throat.
> I am none the wiser. (lines 8–10)

Not only has she not benefited from her devotion, but she realizes that her absorption with her father is isolating her from other relationships, for the rescue that she longs for, the proverbial knight on the white horse. The speaker in the poem is in a state of death-in-life, a state of isolation resulting from her father's death:

> My hours are married to shadow.
> No longer do I listen for the scrape of a keel
> On the blank stones of the landing. (lines 28–30)

The readers of Plath know this shadow. In *The Bell Jar* it is the shadowy cave that Esther crawls into to die in her basement. It is the shadow of the grave, as she makes clear at Joan Gilling's funeral, stating:

> There would be a black, six-foot-deep gap hacked in the hard ground. That shadow would marry this shadow, and the peculiar, yellowish soil of our locality seal the wound in the whiteness, and yet another snowfall erase the traces of newness in Joan's grave. (274)

In their lives, many women are reduced to living in someone else's shadow. To Plath, that shadow is death.

If "The Colossus" portrays the angel, the good daughter sacrificing her life and sublimating her artistry and her passion to better serve the father, "Daddy," of course, portrays the bad daughter, the monster woman who selfishly puts her interests before others. Only an overwhelming anger could break down the barricades of cultural indoctrination and free Plath to express her true feelings. McClatchy says that the poem seems to be a chant or spell "to evoke and exorcise a demon-lover" and concludes that "'Daddy' deals with guilt" (29). But guilt for Plath is just another form of anger, anger turned inward on the victim, locating the cause of the problem within rather than without, in her own rather than another's behavior. Purely speaking, the poem is about anger expressed as an act of rebellion against the tyranny of father and husband, of a patriarchy that stifles her. In an arresting image at the beginning of the poem, Plath calls the patriarchical culture in which she has grown up a

> black shoe
> In which I have lived like a foot
> For thirty years, poor and white,
> Barely daring to breathe or Achoo. (lines 2–5)

Later in the poem, Plath refers to her suicide attempts as efforts to join symbolically with her father in death, stating,

> At twenty I tried to die
> And get back, back, back to you
> I thought even the bones would do. (58–60)

However, as we know, she survives this attempt and is more or less rehabilitated by psychiatric treatment. Plath describes this experience in terms similar to the images of being repaired and retreaded for the road that appear in *The Bell Jar*:

> But they pulled me out of the sack,
> And they stuck me together with glue. (61–2)

Her sense of rehabilitation seems less than perfect; in fact, in *The Bell Jar*, "Daddy," and "Lady Lazarus," Plath makes clear how precarious her sense of identity and mental health are by referring to them constantly as temporary, a patch job that is expected to break down in a matter of time.

In "Daddy" and "Lady Lazarus," men have become Plath's implacable foes, the source of the oppression, which is murdering her. In "Daddy" her father is a devil, "the black man who / Bit my pretty red heart in two" (55–6), her husband "The vampire who said he was you" (72). In "Lady Lazarus," Plath addresses them as Herr Doktor, Herr Enemy. She sees her suffering as a cheap carnival sideshow, her life a source of vicarious pleasure for "The peanut-crunching crowd" (26).

Blessing points out that one of Plath's stylistic devices is beginning *in medias res*. He adds, "No one is better than Plath at giving her reader the experience of being swept up in an action that has been gathering momentum for some time" (60), and such is the beginning of "Lady Lazarus":

> I have done it again.
> One year in every ten
> I manage it—— (1-3)

Blessing says that the use of indefinite pronouns such as "I" and "it" helps Plath to create this effect. The "it" of the poem is the act of suicide which the speaker in the poem attempts each decade: "This is number Three" (22). Again, we have the image of the patched up survivor, a kind of Frankenstein monster or mummy: "They unwrap me hand and foot—— /"The big strip tease" (28-29). Dying is an art that the woman has learned to do well; it is her special calling, but the triumph of a job well done expressed in the poem is bitterly cynical in its irony.

The woman's only means of expression is through her own body, and to do very, very well a task not of her own choosing. According to Gilbert and Gubar in *The Madwoman in the Attic*:

> From Anne Finch's Ardelia, who struggles to escape the male designs in which she feels herself enmeshed to Sylvia Plath's "Lady Lazarus," who tells "Herr Doktor...Herr Enemy" that "I am your opus, / I am your valuable," the woman writer acknowledges with pain, confusion, and anger that what she sees in the mirror is usually a male construct, the "pure gold baby" of male brains, a glittering and wholly artificial child. (18)

If Plath is a Frankenstein's monster born of male vanity, in "Lady Lazarus" she certainly intends for men to pay. She writes:

> There is a charge
> For the eyeing of my scars, there is a charge
> For the hearing of my heart——
> It really goes.
> And there is a charge, a very large charge,
> For a word or a touch
> Or a bit of blood
> Or a piece of my hair or my clothes. (57–64)

First, Plath sees herself as a parallel to the Christian martyrs made saints, with her body becoming a relic, presumably capable of performing miracles. But there is not enough satisfaction in being just a relic, a work of men, an idol to be worshipped, so she espouses the myth of the phoenix:

> Out of the ash
> I rise with my red hair
> And I eat men like air. (82–84)

Obviously, Plath's Lady Lazarus is a monster back from the dead, a witch or the female equivalent of the bogeyman, a myth intended to threaten men.

In "Daddy" and "Lady Lazarus," Plath attempts to transform herself from passive victim to active avenger, to project her deeply-rooted self-hatred outward toward the men in her life who appear to be the source of her low self-esteem. But her tantrum remains unconvincing. Ostriker writes of Plath's intent in these two poems:

> Think of the bravado of the last line [of "Daddy"]: "Daddy, Daddy, you bastard, I'm through," where "through" should mean she has successfully punctured him ("a stake in your fat black heart"), is finished with her attachment to him, and has emerged from something like a tunnel. We believe her not at all. The more she screams the more we know she will never be through. It is the same with the famous ending of "Lady Lazarus," where the poet warns she will rise from the dead and "eat men like air." [H]er incantation is hollow. She is impersonating a female Phoenix–fiend like a woman wearing a Halloween costume
> She is powerless, she knows it, she hates it. (49)

In these poems, Plath is momentarily able to assume the role of the aggressor, but that persona appears in a distinct minority of the poems in *Ariel*. Plath's "sense of herself" concludes Susan Van Dyne, "seems to depend on gaining recognition from the other. Her anxious assertions demand confirmation, but she seems to expect only denial" (140-41). Plath always sees herself as the shadow of the person she wishes to be.

As a symbol of aggression and empowerment, Plath's Lady Lazarus appears with her red hair, as in the poem "Stings" the powerful queen bee is portrayed as:

> ...flying
> More terrible than she ever was, red
> Scar in the sky, red comet
> Over the engine that killed her——
> The mausoleum, the wax house. (56-60)

Red is a highly symbolic color in the writings of women. White represents women's outward passivity and purity in conformation to patriarchical culture, but red represents the creative life force within, the menstrual flow symbolic of the mature woman. Red and white appear over and over in Plath's poems like the turning of a barber's pole, as Plath is torn between what she perceives as her duty and her individuality.

A brilliant example of this red-white imagery appears in "Tulips," another poem in *Ariel.* Anne Stevenson in her biography of Plath, describes the "menacing imagery" of "Tulips," written ten days after Plath left the hospital in February 1961 following an appendectomy (210). According to her husband, Ted Hughes, it was her "first spontaneous poem. She wrote it quickly, without recourse to her thesaurus, and it combines exactness of observation with the subjectivity of her hidden, deeper voice" (qtd. in Stevenson 210). The poem describes a woman in the hospital who identifies the whiteness and sterility of the setting with purification and death. A gift of red tulips is seen as marring the mood with a violent burst of color associated with assertiveness and life. The woman sees the tulips as forcing her unwillingly back to life.

In the poems in *Ariel,* Plath generally presents in a negative light everyday common objects that would normally be comforting. In "Tulips" for example, the speaker's patent leather overnight case becomes a threatening black pillbox, and the smiles in her family photo are fishhooks that catch her skin, causing her pain. In the same vein, a common, thoughtful gift of flowers becomes in the poem a source of anxiety and danger. She states,

> The tulips should be behind bars like dangerous animals;
> They are opening like the mouth of some great African cat,
> And I am aware of my heart: it opens and closes
> Its bowl of red blooms out of sheer love of me. (58-61)

Plath's theme in "Tulips" is that passivity and death are not only preferable to life but morally superior to it, a point she makes obvious when she states, "I am Vertical / But I would rather be horizontal" (1-2) in the poem. "I am Vertical."

As does Chopin in *The Awakening,* Plath's *Ariel* seems methodically to identify and analyze various paths available to women in life and find them without satisfaction or comfort. No wonder Plath's works often hinge upon the purity of the newborn baby, as in the conclusion of the poem "Getting There":

> And I, stepping from this skin

Of old bandages, boredom, old faces
Step to you from the black car of Lethe,
Pure as a baby. (65-68)

If, as Barnard concludes about this poem, the "there" where Plath is getting, the destination, is death, then obviously through death Plath hopes to be reborn, this time as a whole person, not one glued together (79). Commenting on this common theme in Plath's work, Jon Rosenblatt observes:

> her poems frequently perceive of death not as a suicidal ending but as the path to a transformed identity. This point is of particular importance because the common critical tendency is to view Plath solely as a poet of suicide. Actually, her imagery and the characteristic movement of her poems dramatize a death-and-rebirth pattern in much the same way that her novel, *The Bell Jar*, embodies a psychic death and regeneration. (27)

Sandra M. Gilbert interprets this pattern in slightly different terms in "'A Fine, White Flying Myth': Confessions of a Plath Addict":

> Being enclosed—in plaster, in a bell jar, a cellar or a waxhouse—and then being liberated from an enclosure by a maddened or suicidal or "hairy and ugly" avatar of the self is, I would contend, at the heart of the myth that we piece together from Plath's poetry, fiction, and life, just as it is at the heart of much other important writing by nineteenth- and twentieth-century women. The story told is invariably a story of being trapped, by society or by the self as an agent of society, and then somehow escaping or trying to escape. (55)

At its most optimistic interpretation, this death is linked with some kind of rebirth.

However, as Gilbert points out, the key idea is to simply escape, whether or not rebirth is an option. One motif evident in Plath's, as well as Chopin's work, is an escape backward into a prelapsarian childhood before the contamination of adult sexuality, a retreat that Gilbert calls "a rebirth into the imagined liberty of childhood" (57). Such is the conclusion of *The Awakening*, which allows Gilbert to interpret the ending of that novel as a rebirth for Edna. And such is the connotation of much of the baby imagery in *The Bell Jar* and *Ariel*. But always in Plath's work, there is a need for escape that overpowers the wishful thinking of rebirth, and, as the reader moves through the poems in *Ariel*, a sense of finality and doom gathers, a sense which is represented by the poems "Death & Co." and "Edge."

In contrast to the death-rebirth motif, the poem "Death & Co." seems to portray death as a dead end. Utilizing the *in medias res* technique, Plath starts,

> Two, of course, there are two
> It seems perfectly natural now—— (1-2)

The two are two representations of death that Plath, in explaining the poem during an interview, says are "two men, two business friends, who have come to call" (qtd. in Blessing 62). One is a vulture, with "The nude / Verdigris of the condor" whose "beak / Claps sideways" (8-11). She has not yet become his victim, but always there is the murmuring at her ear, like the sea sounds that Edna Pontellier hears, a siren's song of death. He speaks to her in terms, which seem designed especially to demoralize a woman: "He tells me how badly I photograph" (12). This grotesque vision of death as a vulture is hideous, but it is not hypocritical.

It is the other face of death that Plath finds especially revolting. Appearing not just human but even alluring, it is the one who smiles and smokes: "He wants to be loved" (25) by his victims. To him death is a game, a form of sexual seduction. Blessing compares this image of death with "the seductive courtier of Dickinson's 'Because I could not stop for Death' " (62-63). The speaker in the poem does not stir, hiding in passivity, but even so she hears the dead bell and knows "Somebody's done for" (31). In "Death & Co.," Plath is merely evading death temporarily, but it is the concluding act of a weary struggle. The reader surely knows that it is only a matter of time before the speaker succumbs to the ever present enticements of death, which are summarized so well in "Tulips":

> To lie with my hands turned up and be utterly empty.
> How free it is, you have no idea how free——
> The peacefulness is so big it dazes you,
> And it asks nothing, a nametag, a few trinkets.
> It is what the dead close on, finally; I imagine them
> Shutting their mouths on it, like a Communion tablet. (30-35)

In her critical biography of Plath, Harriet Rosenstein remarks on the constant use Plath makes of oral imagery in her poetry such as that in the lines cited above from "Tulips":

> Plath's late poetry is full of mouths, open, demanding, never satisfied. Those of children, of flowers, of animals, of other women, of men, and of her speakers. One's sense always is that the universe is insatiable because the speaker herself is insatiable. (qtd. in Maris 131)

It is Plath's insatiable appetite that makes the peace and cessation of want, which she associates with death, appear so enticing to her. Rosenstein concludes:

> No amount of food, real or symbolic, can fill the emptiness within. And every demand from outside threatens to deplete her still further, provocations thus to terror or rage. Her fate—her dissolution—has in this and many other poems the ring of inevitability. (qtd. in Maris 131)

In one of her earlier poems in *Ariel*, "Years," Plath writes:

> Eternity bores me,
> I never wanted it.
> What I love is
> The piston in motion. (9–12)

However, by the end of *Ariel*, by the time she writes "Edge," to the tormented Plath, such peace looks like heaven.

Many critics consider *Ariel* to be one long suicide note culminating in "Edge," a poem which feminist critic Paula Bennett characterizes as Plath's "last, bleakest, and perhaps most perfect poem" (150). "Edge" has received a great deal of critical attention, but nobody has developed a reading that accounts for all of the poem's elements. Because critics may have been reluctant to deal directly and objectively with female sexuality, a consistent interpretation of the poem as a whole has not been presented.

In analyzing Plath's poetry in general, Harold Bloom and other critics fault her for being too sensational, too subjective, and for offering images which appear personal and, as a result, arbitrary. She developed such an idiosyncratic system of symbol and myth that Arthur Oberg in "Sylvia Plath and the New Decadence" concludes of her work, "after long inspection, [her poems] remain unfamiliar and increasingly disdainful of outer, human reference. In the history of poetry, language has seldom been so evidently in crisis, written so painfully *in extremis*" (178). Annette Lavers says that Plath's meanings "can be extremely cryptic if one is not aware of their derivation" (111), while McClatchy feels that her best poems are those whose "lines are pared down at times to a stark, private code" (90). In Plath's defense, Ted Hughes states that many of her later poems "seem to be constructed of arbitrary surreal symbols [but] are really impassioned reorganizations of relevant fact" (qtd. in Broe 2). Judith Kroll sums up by saying that "In Plath's late poems, hallucinatory or surreal elements qualify the psychological drama, but the poems never descend into the merely fantastic" (26). All of these comments fit "Edge," in one way or another, but the poem is finally simpler and more direct than critics have made it out to be.

A perfect climax to Plath's later poetry, "Edge" deals with a dead woman's body, first externally and then internally with her reproductive and sexual organs. The poem may be seen as Plath's combination suicide note and autopsy. An analysis of the themes and images of "Edge" in these terms helps to account for the poem's profound impact and power, as well as to shed light on Plath's objective, distanced attitude toward a woman's suicide, and ultimately upon her own suicide.

"Edge" is parallel in imagery and theme to much of Plath's later poetry. Most of the poems comprising *Ariel* were completed within four months, resulting in "a high degree of consistency in thematic and imagistic elements in the late poems" (Rosenblatt 88). As we have seen, Plath was obsessed with the themes of death (particularly by suicide), the achievement of perfection, and the concept of rebirth. Her images are frequently drawn from contemporary and classical references or from the female body, and she uses the moon as the central pivotal symbol of her cosmic mythology. "Edge" is a cool, perfect culmination of those themes and images, a perfect ending poem of her work.

Critics who have analyzed the poem have focused first on Plath's representation of death as a state of perfection, a theme similarly employed by Wallace Stevens, a poet who greatly influenced Plath's work. Plath's writings often focus on a need to achieve perfection or purity and on death as a state of perfection: "Edge" begins by stating that the woman is perfected in death. Lavers notes that to Plath "purification can be achieved in death, in which the scattered personality is seen as gradually withdrawing toward its vital center and abandoning its tainted externals" (128), and in "Edge" we find that the body in death withdraws, implodes to its core, the reproductive organs. In a telling incident, Plath wrote in her journal about a dead bird being "composed, perfect and beautiful in death" (qtd. in Wagner-Martin 153). Although in her poem "The Munich Mannequins" Plath exclaims that "Perfection is terrible, it cannot have children" (1), according to John Romano, her work more characteristically evinces "The recurring desire for cleanliness and purity...[which] is really the desire not to have a body at all, and manifests itself in disgust with all bodily functions, especially sex" (50). Romano concludes that Plath's extreme viewpoint left her with "only the choice between a cold, still death and a 'bed of fire.' The sardonic triumph of the former is recorded in 'Edge'" (51).

That "Her dead / Body wears a smile of accomplishment" (2-3) is both literal and ironic at the same time. Plath sees death as an accomplishment and a release from the struggles of life, but with the verb "wears," there is a hint of the plastic smiles worn by women in the kinds of advertising that appears in *Mademoiselle* magazine, women who are forced into playing a part in society as serene objects of art for male artists. One of Plath's conflicts in life was between being true to her individuality and unusual talent and being loved and admired as a stereotypical woman. Only in death is Plath able to resolve this conflict and reach a state of perfection by destroying the mind and soul, leaving only the body. As Edward Butscher notes, "The dead woman is now herself a work of art" (362). Thus, the woman in her poem has become the static, plastic model, the mannequin, which society often tells a woman to be. Romano confirms that such perfection "is achieved, moreover, with 'the illusion of a Greek necessity,' that is as if our state were naturally and necessarily so perfect, which it is not" (51).

In conjunction with Plath's obsession with death as a purifying experience, is her parallel theme of rebirth. As previously discussed, the concept of rebirth is apparent in her most famous poems "Daddy" and "Lady Lazarus," but these references do not so much identify the rebirth of a whole individual as the continued survival of a patchwork personality. If Plath initially proposes two ways out of her anguish—rebirth or self-destruction—by the time that she writes "Edge," self-destruction has clearly become the only option. There is not even a hint of rebirth in "Edge." Pamela Annas argues that this poem is "about the attainment of perfection through a stopping process" (121). She goes on to say, "The poem has the quality of a still photograph" (122).

"Edge" is unified with the other poems of *Ariel* not only in theme but in imagery. The key to understanding the poem fully is to understand Plath's imagery. The poem begins with classical allusions by referring to the woman's death shroud as a toga with its drapery like scrolls, both a visual image and an allusion to Plath's volumes of written work. Her feet are bare because she is dead and is a pilgrim who has finished the pilgrimage of life. There is also the image of the seeker after divine truth, humble before the altar. She has reached her destiny: "We have come so far, it is over" (8).

Critics have found other allusions. Both Judith Kroll and Shanta Acharya have extensively documented the similarities between the woman in the poem and Shakespeare's Cleopatra. Acharya, pointing out that Cleopatra calls the asp with which she commits suicide her baby at her breast, finds a parallel in Plath's lines about "a white serpent, / One at each little / pitcher of milk, now empty" (9-11) and adds that Cleopatra also saw death as a means of perfection (54). Cleopatra accepts her fate with stoic resignation and, therefore, ennobles herself, as does the speaker in "Edge." In addition to the allusion to Cleopatra, the poem may contain an allusion to Medea, who killed her two children in an act of spite against Jason who had cast her off. Plath would obviously be drawn to a myth that allowed her to act out her anger against her husband who had abandoned her and the two babies. Following the Classical statuary imagery as they do, these lines may very well be referring to Cleopatra and Medea, but I find here a more direct and simpler reading; for it is with these lines that the poem shifts from describing the external body of the woman to the internal—to the reproductive and the sexual organs.

Lines 9 through 20 develop an extended metaphor, a technique Plath makes extensive use of in her poetry, and as noted by Arthur Oberg in *Modern American Lyric: Lowell, Berryman, Creeley, and Plath,* "In many of the late poems, she directed her relentless precision toward casting poems in the form of extended correlatives...Each poem exposes a search for [the] adequate image" (139). That adequate image in "Edge" is the woman's own body. One theme of "Edge" is the achievement of perfection by the withdrawal of the individual from life and its corrupting compromises. Plath describes this withdrawal in bodily terms, comparing the female reproductive organs to a rose in a garden, which is apt since a rose is literally a set of reproductive organs. Plath frequently refers to the female body, and in poems such as "Cut" and "Edge," Plath extends the concept of the landscape technique to the female body: "The landscape becomes a 'bodyscape'; the poet treats the body as if it were external to her self" (Rosenblatt 101).

With the image of the female reproductive and sexual organs in mind, the troublesome rest of the poem comes into clearer focus. Plath speaks of "Each dead child coiled, a white serpent, / One at each little / Pitcher of milk, now empty" (9-11). Whereas interpretations of these lines as an allusion to the Medea myth, the children as literally Plath's two children, or even as a reference to her poems as children are helpful, to take them as final and inclusive would be to ignore the unity of imagery an alternative reading suggests. The children may be the ovaries, the point of origin for her two biological children, and the white serpents the fallopian tubes. In death the woman "has folded / them back into her body as petals / of a rose close" (12-14). As the rose closes in upon itself in death, so her essential identity as a woman—her reproductive organs—closes up at the end of her life. They have fulfilled their function in reproducing—one girl and one boy—to replace their parents. Her reproductive destiny has been fulfilled, and she is biologically expendable. The paradox of literal and ironic tone is carried forward in the poem by the fact that Plath is only thirty and still fertile. However, perfection is stasis, balance, and can have no more children. If death-in-life is a theme in much of her later poetry, in "Edge" the theme is life-in-death with the folding up of the fertile reproductive organs and the teeming, productive mind.

The simile of the rose shifts our attention from the reproductive to the sexual. When Plath writes, "as petals / Of a rose close when the garden / Stiffens and odors bleed / From the sweet, deep throat of the night flower" (13-16), what could have been an erotic, alluring vaginal image is undercut by the use of the words "bleed" suggesting menstruation and "stiffens" suggesting dried blood, rigor mortis, and decay.

Plath then states that "The moon has nothing to be sad about, / Staring from her hood of bone" (17-18). The moon corresponds to the uterus hiding behind the pelvic bone, the uterus whose cycle is, of course, said to be governed by the moon. Plath also says in her poem "The Moon and the Yew Tree" that "the moon is my mother" (17), which it figuratively is. Her womb and its reproductive function link her to her mother and every other woman. The moon is a useful symbol to Plath. Lavers explains:

> White is also the absence of colour, and is indeed the symbol of death in some civilizations. This coupled with the other attributes of death, makes the moon the perfect symbol for it: it shines in the night, its light is borrowed, its shape regular, well-defined and self-contained, and its bald light turns everything into stone. The moon is also a suitable symbol for sterility because of its circular shape, the most perfect of all, and because it rules the flux of menstrual blood. In the latter death is in the midst of life, which is cut from its rightful end, according to Sylvia Plath. (109-10)

Kroll concludes, "It is no exaggeration to say that the symbol of the Moon is structurally indispensable to the late poems" (79) and "If 'The Moon and the Yew Tree' were taken to be the first of the late poems, they could be said to begin and end with this relation to the moon" (44). The moon is Plath's personal muse. To her, "there was both a 'woman in the moon' and one out of it" (Kroll 63). In "Edge," the moon-muse and Plath as the moon are looking on with complete detachment on the final rite of purification—death.

The poem's final two lines are: "She is used to this sort of thing. / Her blacks crackle and drag" (19-20). The moon is inconstant and used to change. It takes all things in stride, both life and death as it waxes and wanes in its perpetual cycle. The final line has been the most problematic of all. Critics have tried to explain it in terms of the moon, or they simply quote the line and let it stand as though quoting were explaining. But if we read the "her" as being the woman's body, as indeed Plath's own body, then the reference is to her pubis with the black hairs that crackle and drag towards a reluctant closure. This reading culminates the body imagery and unifies the last half of the poem around the extended metaphor, and this reference to her pubic hair parallels the other extended metaphor in the poem of the flower in the garden since the hairs call to mind the filament-like stamens of the flower.

Thus "Edge" is organized around a description of the author's own body in death. Externally the point of view is objective and distanced, much like that of a coroner examining a corpse. Internally, the focus is upon the woman as a reproductive being, withdrawing from the imperatives of biology. While Margaret Newlin sees in the poem, "The sense of recklessness, of teetering with wild gaiety on the edge of an abyss" (367), A. Alvarez concludes that Plath "went to the extreme, far edge of the bearable and, in the end, slipped over" (17).

David Holbrook in *Sylvia Plath: Poetry and Existence* is horrified and appalled by the images and themes of "Edge" because he feels that the poem "is beautiful but psychotic" (271). He argues that to appreciate the poem is to be oblivious to its moral implications—suicide and infanticide. However, his reaction shows a failure to understand the themes and images of the poem. First, Plath was not at all proposing the killing of her children, but moreover, it is hypocritical to hold her solely accountable for the welfare of the children. She and her children are victims of a society that allows fathers to abandon their wives and children with impunity. Even if "Edge" contains overtones from the Medea myth, a point, which I reject, then Plath is only acting out the logical conclusion of a society which considers the welfare of its women and children to be superfluous to the attainment of male achievement.

Plath is dealing in "Edge," and in the rest of *Ariel*, with the most basic philosophical conundrum—the meaning of life in the face of eventual death. Plath might object that she did not choose suicide but had it chosen for her as the only means society allowed her to exert active control over her own life. In this respect "Edge" parallels the conclusion of Chopin's *The Awakening* where Edna sees her two children as societal traps requiring her to sacrifice her selfhood. Edna, too, sees suicide as her only choice to break the cycle of birth, death, and obligation. Perhaps the moral implications of "Edge" and the other poems in *Ariel* are derived from a society that often does not support genius in a woman and places unequal responsibilities on women for the maintenance of its most basic unit—the family.

Elizabeth Hardwick suggests that for Plath, her life and her work are ultimately and inexorably mixed:

> She, the poet, is frighteningly there all the time. Orestes rages, but Aeschylus lives
> to be almost seventy. Sylvia Plath, however, is both heroine and author; when the
> curtain goes down, it is her own dead body there on the stage, sacrificed to her
> plot. (102)

What critics of Plath often allude to is the troubling problem of persona in Plath's work. Can the work be separated from the artist, from biography, as the formalist critical theory dictates? Such a separation appears to be unattainable in Plath's case. Arguments that the speaker in Plath's poems is not really Plath herself seem to be unconvincing, and for a very good reason: for Sylvia Plath, the image which she projected to the external world was her carefully constructed persona. Her efforts to be the perfect daughter, wife, and mother were creations to cover the real person inside. This person which is not a persona but the real Plath, is the speaker in the poems, reversing the standard conception of person and persona.

Therefore, the pain evinced in Plath's work is all the more terrible for its reality, without the cool eye of artistic objectivity to provide a comforting distance. Unsympathetic to Plath's pain, Calvin Bedient in "Sylvia Plath, Romantic" concludes of her life and works, "Far from being a tragedy of will, like classical tragedy, Plath's is a tragedy of weakness, of a fatal vulnerability to the sense of injury" (14). Bedient misunderstands the Greek necessity that brought Plath to her death, a destiny independent of will, weakness, or action, a point Judith Kroll makes when she states:

> Plath's dying heroines, in poems such as "A Birthday Present" and "Edge," have
> little in common with stereotypes of suicidal women (in whose actions a sense of
> the meaning of death does not even figure), and a great deal in common with tragic
> heroines who die calmly and nobly. (148)

Like Oedipus, the more Plath struggles, the more she is trapped. Her fate has been predetermined not by her life but by an accident of birth, her gender.

Sylvia Plath's obsession with suicide makes her, of course, the perfect subject for a study of women's suicide in literature. While Kate Chopin employed suicide as a literary device, Plath took the final step beyond art and committed suicide. Obviously, Plath's work is more completely possessed with the notion of suicide, but it is Chopin who presents the most completely positive view of the subject. Chopin broke the male Romantic paradigm of presenting female suicides in literature as resulting from mental illness and *mal d'amour.* Edna Pontellier is never more sane than when she swims out into infinity. But ultimately, this is a literary device, a construct to be interpreted and debated, ignored or celebrated as times or cultures change. Plath was working somewhere else. Was Sylvia Plath mentally ill? That indeed is the question. Her actions and those of her personae elicit a wide range of possible answers. At the end, however, it seems evident that Plath's view of suicide is not far from Chopin's. The death portrayed in "Edge" is certainly visionary not violent and does not seem to be instigated by mental illness or *mal d'amour.* The awful precision with which Plath shuts down her own body has no parallel in literature; the joy of death seems unique to Plath.

CHAPTER V

Conclusion:
A Room Is Not Enough

In the study of feminist literary criticism, it often seems that all roads lead to Virginia Woolf. With publication of *A Room of One's Own* in 1929, Woolf becomes one of the first feminist literary critics. This work provides important philosophical underpinning to feminist literary criticism by defining the limitations that exist for women artists, limitations that their male counterparts do not have to face. In the process, Woolf also defines many of the same barriers that continue to prevent women in the twenty-first century from achieving personal freedom. Rather than continuing to apologize for women and begging for better treatment, Woolf's work demands more recognition and opportunities for women.

However, as we have seen with her contemporaries, Wharton and Chopin, Woolf was not comfortable with the label of feminist, her ambivalence towards it probably representative of the same reservations that Wharton and Chopin had. According to Alex Zwerdling, Woolf internalized the cultural norms of her age to such an extent that she could not come to grips with the rage exhibited by Plath that is at the heart of feminism, at least as feminism has developed in the latter half of the twentieth century. Woolf's reticence towards her anger is noted by Adrienne Rich in her landmark essay "When We Dead Awaken: Writing as Re-Vision" published in 1971:

> In rereading Virginia Woolf's *A Room of One's Own* for the first time in some years, I was astonished at the sense of effort, of pains taken, of dogged tentativeness, in the tone of that essay. And I recognized that tone. I had heard it often enough, in myself and in other women. It is the tone of a woman almost in touch with her anger, who is determined not to appear angry, who is *willing* herself to be calm, detached, and even charming in a roomful of men where things have been said which are attacks on her very integrity.
>
> S]he was trying to sound as cool as Jane Austen, as Olympian as Shakespeare, because that is the way the men of the culture thought a writer should sound. (37)

In other words, these writers—Woolf, Chopin, and Wharton—were haunted by the specter of the monster image which patriarchical society had created.

Between that image and the dichotomy of sanity/insanity that results from the Age of Reason, it would take an extremely secure woman to embrace a movement that from the point of view of social norms at the turn of the century bordered on hysteria. Echoing Rich, Zwerdling argues that in *A Room of One's Own*, Woolf was attempting "to find a vehicle to accommodate her twin needs" which were "to vent her anger about the subjection of women and to conciliate the male audience she could never entirely ignore" (243). The societal reasons fueling these contradictory impulses have already been amply illustrated, but Woolf also had to contend with the current fashion in literary criticism. According to Zwerdling,

> The whole literary climate of Woolf's time fostered the kind of detached, controlled, impersonal esthetic theory she adopted. It was a standard by which she regularly judged her fellow writers, male as well as female. Woolf would have had little sympathy with anyone who recommended that she get in closer touch with her own anger. She *was* in close touch with it; to have put those feelings on more prominent display would not, to her way of thinking, have produced better art; on the contrary. (247)

If the first impulse now is to damn Woolf for her cautiousness and cultural cowardice, Rich defends her and many other women writers in observing,

> No male writer has written primarily or even largely for women, or with the sense of women's criticism as a consideration when he chooses his materials, his theme, his language. But to a lesser or greater extent, every woman writer has written for men even when, like Virginia Woolf, she was supposed to be addressing women. (37-38)

Woolf cannot be especially criticized for an approach, which has been the Procrustes's bed of women's art. If in the context of the 1890s, we found Chopin's break with the paradigm of the romantic novel to be both revolutionary and unrewarding, in the area of women directly expressing in their work the rage they feel, it is Sylvia Plath who first breaks that ground. Rich declares that in Plath's work "a subjective, personal rage blazes forth, never before seen in women's poetry. If it is unnerving it is also cathartic, the blowtorch of language cleansing the rust and ticky-tacky and veneer from an entire consciousness" (qtd. in Gelpi and Gelpi xii).

Even if we conclude in the first decade of the twenty-first century that Woolf's thoughts might be some of that "ticky-tacky" which might ultimately have to be outgrown, still, in 1929 she made important contributions to the burgeoning women's movement. In *A Room of One's Own*, Woolf argues that in order to create, the woman artist needs isolation and security—a room of her own and 500 pounds a year income. Although the book initially focuses on the specific needs of the female as artist, Woolf's subject leads her to explore the situation for women in general. Woolf compares the mythical male university of Oxbridge to a sister institution of higher education for women. While the university provides every means of support to the male students in their pursuit of achievement, the women have to do with meager resources. The reason for this discrepancy, according to Woolf, is that the men in the family control the accumulation and distribution of wealth, while the women are limited to those roles in a patriarchical society dictated by the reproductive function.

Woolf explores the consequences of these limitations in the fable of Judith Shakespeare, the fantasy sister of the great playwright. This fable is Woolf's answer to the question of "why no woman wrote a word of that extraordinary [Elizabethan] literature when every other man, it seemed, was capable of song or sonnet" (43). Thus she invents Judith, a woman "as adventurous, as imaginative, as agog to see the world as he [Shakespeare] was" (49). Of course, Judith's talents elicit a completely different response from her family than those of her brother, William. First of all, there is no question of her attending school, "no chance of learning grammar and logic, let alone of reading Horace and Virgil" (49). Her education is piecemeal, picked up from the droppings of her brother's. Her fate is to make herself useful around the house until a suitable marriage can be arranged for her, normally at an early age. When that marriage is arranged, Judith rebels, first declaring "that marriage was hateful to her" (49) and having received no reprieve, running away from home as a last resort. Woolf does not specify what is so hateful about marriage for a woman of talent, but Adrienne Rich does:

> Now, to be maternally with small children all day in the old way, to be with a man in the old way of marriage, requires a holding-back, a putting-aside of that imaginative activity, and demands instead a kind of conservatism. [T]o be a female human being trying to fulfill traditional female functions in a traditional way *is* in direct conflict with the subversive function of the imagination. (43)

Rich here echoes Esther Greenwood's fears in *The Bell Jar*, the fear that marriage and children will undermine her creative ability and remove her individuality, leaving behind her double, the numb slave in a private totalitarian state.

So like her brother before her, Woolf's Judith goes to London to be on the stage, but her reception there is no different than at home, for ironically women then did not have the privilege to engage in what would later still be an unrespectable vocation for them—acting. Woolf has Judith end up pregnant by Nick Greene, the actor–manager of the troupe, a tragedy which prompts Woolf to ask, "who shall measure the heat and violence of the poet's heart when caught and tangled in a woman's body?" (50), a question particularly apt for Plath. Woolf ends her fable on an ironic note, stating that Judith "killed herself one winter's night and lies buried at some cross-roads where the omnibuses now stop outside the Elephant and Castle" (50). In the end, Judith's heat and violence are not transmuted into art, unless her subsequent suicide can be called art, replicating yet again "the pernicious act of self-destruction" Gilbert and Gubar find to be the companion to female self-assertion (*Madwoman* 42). Thus Woolf concludes:

> ...any woman born with a great gift in the sixteenth century would certainly have gone crazed, shot herself, or ended her days in some lonely cottage outside the village, half witch, half wizard, feared and mocked at. For it needs little skill in psychology to be sure that a highly gifted girl who had tried to use her gift for poetry would have been so thwarted and hindered by other people, so tortured and pulled asunder by her own contrary instincts, that she must have lost her health and sanity to a certainty. (51)

Although Woolf ascribes these events specifically to the mind set of the Elizabethan age, there is no reason to conclude that the fable would unfold very differently in Woolf's own time. Perhaps Woolf revealed more than she thought in her analysis of the plight of Judith Shakespeare because Woolf, of course, also ended up committing suicide in 1941 by weighting herself down with stones and drowning herself in a river. She did this ostensibly as a result of her mental illness which she feels, as her suicide note reflects, makes her a burden to her husband: "I am doing what seems the best thing to do...I know I am spoiling your life, that without me you could work" (qtd. in Bell 226). It is difficult to imagine a man leaving such a note.

But what of the idea that women need a room of their own to make fulfillment possible? In *The Awakening*, Kate Chopin has her protagonist, Edna Pontellier, attempt to establish a room of her own, first in her house, and then in a separate residence called the Pigeon House. But as the novel progresses, isolation does not alleviate Edna's problem. The isolation of a room does not work because it is first of all incomplete, and more importantly, women do not fundamentally wish to be isolated from society but rather recognized by it and accepted for what they are. No matter how well intended, ultimately, the concept of having a room of one's own smacks of its racial equivalent of "separate but equal": a philosophy doomed to failure because the separate never becomes equal. However, the fundamental fallacy of this approach lies in a hidden assumption underpinning Woolf's concept—why must a woman be limited to claiming only one room in what is ostensibly her own house? The answer is, of course, that the house is only nominally hers; in fact, it is owned and controlled by her husband. Therefore, it is at her husband's sufferance that she is allowed to claim one room as hers, and what he gives, he can at any time take away. These limitations to the concept of having a room of one's own are illustrated by Doris Lessing in her short story "To Room 19."

"To Room 19" is another work by a woman artist in which the action moves inexorably towards suicide as its conclusion. The basic plot of the story is strikingly similar to *The Awakening*: an upper-middle-class married woman with children finds after several years of marriage that the traditional female roles of wife and mother are stifling. Mona Knapp writes,

> The story traces the fate of a woman who does everything "intelligently," from her well-matched and timely marriage to the wisely spaced children, to the sensibly mortgaged house in the suburbs. As required by the patriarchical rule by which she abides, Susan gives up her own apartment to marry, and then her profession to raise her children. In her mid-forties, she stands at the center of a complicated configuration of household and parental duties, community ties, possessions, payments, and social engagements. (79)

Despite having satisfied all of the societal demands on her, she can find no satisfaction in her life. As Knapp notes, "She is ruined by the very achievement of her goal" (79).

Lessing ironically starts the story by stating that it is "about a failure in intelligence" (164). The Rawlingses have been intelligent and rational in every decision they have made—a rationality that is predicated upon the assumptions of a patriarchical society. By society's standards, Susan begins to go slowly insane, as we have seen Edna Pontellier and Esther Greenwood so judged. As she herself notes, "there was something really wrong with her" (175). Following the "rational" dictates of society, she had selflessly given up her own identity in the service of her children and husband. But as Gilbert and Gubar observe, "To be trained in renunciation is almost necessarily to be trained to ill health, since the human animal's first and strongest urge is to his/her *own* survival, pleasure, assertion" (*Madwoman* 54). In fact, Susan is not going insane but is finally gaining her sanity in an insane world, or as Chopin describes this awakening for Edna, "She felt like some new-born creature, opening its eyes in a familiar world it had never known" (340).

Susan at first struggles against her new vision; she protests, "She had never felt marriage, or the children, as bondage. Neither had he [her husband], or surely they wouldn't be together lying in each other's arms content after twelve years of marriage" (Lessing 175). But, of course, they are not content. He seeks fulfillment in his job and mistress, while Susan's restlessness is driving her ceaselessly forward. Carol Pearson and Katherine Pope write in *The Female Hero in American and British Literature*, "Specifically, the Rawlings' intelligence never took into consideration how far the role of housewife and mother systematically undermines a woman's identity" (48). Susan initially thinks that she is "an irrational person" (Lessing 175), but as the story evolves, she accepts the fact that she has rights as a human being also.

As a solution to her problem, she attempts to create for herself a separate world by literally getting a room of her own, first in her house, and failing at that, in some nondescript boarding house where she goes daily to do nothing but create herself as a separate being. However, despite the fact that her family no longer needs her—the children have an au pair girl, the husband has a mistress, and the house has a maid—they will not let her go, presumably because the family image requires a devoted wife and mother to maintain appearances. When her husband locates her secret room, Susan realizes that her family will never let her go. Failing in her efforts to in some way completely separate herself from her family, to achieve individuality, she commits suicide.

In *The Awakening*, "To Room 19," and *Ariel*, and to a certain extent in *The Bell Jar*, the women protagonists go through strikingly similar emotional journeys. That all of these women come from the upper-middle-class is significant: in their lives, these upper-middle-class women have worked past the needs of survival and security on a physical level. Their need now is for self-actualization, the one fulfillment denied to them. In their search for self-actualization, the protagonists in *The Awakening* and "To Room 19" initially seek a separate, ascetic existence which they believe will somehow purify them and allow them some autonomy within an essentially corrupt society, a concept which Esther Greenwood also works towards in *The Bell Jar*. Unlike Esther, however, Edna, Susan, and the personae in *Ariel* have procreated, already had children, and this fact appears to be a permanent birthmark that cannot be removed. They have already engaged in the essential female function and have contributed to the continuation of the cycle of birth and death that maintains the patriarchical society. The implication one derives from these writers' works is that nothing their protagonists do can relieve them of their bondage, and therefore suicide is the only course open to them for complete control of their lives. They must sacrifice their lives in order finally to gain them.

In the final analysis, they martyr themselves rather than compromise their ideals. In this respect, George Spangler is correct when he says of Edna Pontellier:

> Finally there is a disturbing, even alienating ruthlessness about Edna, but a ruthlessness which eludes moral categories because it is no more and no less than the reflection of her passionate nature's drive for fulfillment. (251)

Spangler's comment is also true of Plath's persona in *Ariel* and of Susan Rawlings in "To Room 19." All of these women characters are driven forward by their desire for autonomy toward a wall of restraints and oppression designed by society to hold women in. In the end, these characters would make any sacrifice to get to the other side.

BIBLIOGRAPHY

Acharya, Shanta. "An Analysis of Sylvia Plath's 'Edge.'" *The Literary Criterion* 14.3 (1979): 52-7.

Alexander, Paul, ed. *Ariel Ascending*. New York: Harper, 1985.

Alvarez, A. *The Savage God*. New York: Random House, 1971.

Ames, Lois. "Sylvia Plath: A Biographical Note." *The Bell Jar*. Toronto: Bantam Books, 1981. 203-16.

Annas, Pamela J. *A Disturbance in Mirrors: The Poetry of Sylvia Plath*. New York: Greenwood, 1988.

Anderson, Olive. *Suicide in Victorian and Edwardian England*. Oxford: Clarendon, 1987.

Auchincloss, Louis. *Edith Wharton: A Woman in Her Time*. New York: Viking, 1971.

Auerbach, Nina. "Falling Alice, Fallen Women, and Victorian Dream Children." *English Language Notes* 20 (Dec 1982): 46-64.

Barnard, Caroline King. *Sylvia Plath*. Boston: Twayne, 1978.

Bassein, Beth Ann. *Women and Death: Linkages in Western Thought and Literature*. Westport, Conn.: Greenwood, 1984.

Bedient, Calvin. "Sylvia Plath, Romantic." Lane 3-18.

Bell, Quentin. *Virginia Woolf: A Biography*. New York: Harcourt, 1972.

Bennett, Paula. *My Life a Loaded Gun: Female Creativity and Feminist Politics*. Boston: Beacon, 1986.

Blessing, Richard Allen. "The Shape of the Psyche: Vision and Technique in the Late Poems of Sylvia Plath." Lane 57-73.

Bloom, Harold, ed. *Kate Chopin: Modern Critical Views*. New York: Chelsea, 1987.

——. "Introduction." Bloom *Kate Chopin* 1-6.

——, ed. *Sylvia Plath: Modern Critical Views*. New York: Chelsea, 1989.

——. "Introduction." Bloom *Sylvia Plath* 1-4.

Bogarand, Carley Rees. "*The Awakening*: A Refusal to Compromise." *University of Michigan Papers in Women's Studies*. Vol. 2. Ann Arbor: U of Michigan P, 1977.

Bourjaily, Vance. "Victoria Lucas and Elly Higginbottom." Alexander 134-51.

Broe, Mary Lynn. *Protean Poetic: The Poetry of Sylvia Plath*. Columbia: U of Missouri P, 1980.

Butscher, Edward. *Sylvia Plath: Method and Madness*. New York: Seabury, 1976.

——, ed. *Sylvia Plath: The Woman and the Work*. New York: Dodd, Mead, 1977.

Chopin, Kate. *The Awakening*. 1899. Culley 3-114.

——. "Retraction." Culley 159.

Culley, Margaret, ed. *The Awakening*. Norton Critical Edition. New York: Norton, 1976.

——. "The Context of *The Awakening*." Culley 117-9.

——. "Editor's Note." Culley 143-4.

——. "Preface." Culley vii–viii.

Dimock, Wai–chee. "Debasing Exchange: Edith Wharton's *The House of Mirth*." PMLA 100 (1985): 783-93.

Eble, Kenneth. "A Forgotten Novel." *Western Humanities Review* 10.3 (Summer 1956): 261-9. Rpt. in Bloom *Kate Chopin* 7-16.

Ellman, Mary. "*The Bell Jar*—An American Girlhood." Newman 221-6.

Fiedler, Leslie A. *Love and Death in the American Novel*. New York: Stein, 1966.

Flaubert, Gustave. *Madame Bovary*. 1857. Trans. Francis Steegmuller. New York: Modern Library, 1957.

Gates, Barbara T. *Victorian Suicide: Mad Crimes and Sad Histories*. Princeton: Princeton UP, 1988.

Gelpi, Barbara Charlesworth, and Albert Gelpi. "Introduction." *Adrienne Rich's Poetry*. Ed. Gelpi and Gelpi. Norton Critical Edition. New York: Norton, 1975. xi–xiii.

Gilbert, Sandra M. "'A Fine White Flying Myth': Confessions of a Plath Addict." *The Massachusetts Review* 19.3 (1978): 585-603. Rpt. in Bloom *Sylvia Plath* 49-66.

————. "The Second Coming of Aphrodite." *The Kenyon Review* 5.3 (Summer 1983): 42-66. Rpt. in Bloom *Kate Chopin* 89-114.

Gilbert, Sandra M., and Susan Gubar. *The Madwoman in the Attic: The Woman Writer and the Nineteenth Century Imagination*. New Haven: Yale UP, 1984.

————. *Sex Changes*. New Haven: Yale UP, 1989. Vol. 2 of *No Man's Land: The Place of the Woman Writer in the Twentieth Century*. 2 vols. 1988-89.

Gould, Jean. *Modern American Women Poets*. New York: Dodd, Mead, 1984.

Hardwick, Elizabeth. "On Sylvia Plath." Alexander 100-15.

Harris, Mason. "*The Bell Jar*: Review." *West Coast Review* 8 (Oct. 1973): 54-56. Rpt. in Wagner 34-37.

Henley, Katherine. "Death as Option: The Heroine in Nineteenth–Century Fiction." *College Language Association Journal* 25.2 (Dec. 1981): 197-202.

Higonnet, Margaret. "Speaking Silences: Women's Suicide." *The Female Body in Western Culture: Contemporary Perspectives*. Ed. Susan Rubin Suleiman. Cambridge: Harvard UP, 1986. 68-83.

Holbrook, David. *Sylvia Plath: Poetry and Existence*. London: Athlone, 1976.

Howe, Irving. "The Plath Celebration: A Partial Dissent." *The Critical Point of Literature and Culture*. New York: Horizon, 1973. Rpt. in Bloom *Sylvia Plath* 5-15.

Kenner, Hugh. "Sincerity Kills." Lane 33-44.

Knapp, Mona. *Doris Lessing*. New York: Ungar, 1984.

Kroll, Judith. *Chapters in a Mythology: The Poetry of Sylvia Plath*. New York: Harper, 1976.

Lameyer, Gordon. "The Double in Sylvia Plath's *The Bell Jar*." Butscher 143-65.

Lane, Gary, ed. *Sylvia Plath: New Views on the Poetry*. Baltimore: Johns Hopkins UP, 1979.

Lant, Kathleen Margaret. "The Siren of Grand Isle: Adele's Role in *The Awakening*." *Southern Studies: An Interdisciplinary Journal of the South* 23.2 (Summer 1984): 167-75. Rpt. in Bloom *Kate Chopin* 115-24.

Lavers, Annette. "The World as Icon—On Sylvia Plath's Themes." Newman 100-35.

Lessing, Doris. *The Doris Lessing Reader*. New York: Knopf, 1988.

Lowell, Robert. "Foreword." *Ariel by Sylvia Plath*. New York: Harper, 1966. vii-ix.

Maris, Ronald W. *Pathways to Suicide: A Survey of Self–Destructive Behaviors*. Baltimore: Johns Hopkins UP, 1981.

May, John R. "Local Color in *The Awakening*." *The Southern Review* 6 (1970): 1031-40. Rpt. in Culley 189-94.

McClatchy, J. D. "Short Circuits and Folding Mirrors." Lane 19-32.

Milliner, Gladys W. "The Tragic Imperative: *The Awakening* and *The Bell Jar*." *Mary Wollstonecraft Newspaper* Dec. 1973: 21-26.

Modleski, Tania. *Loving with a Vengeance: Mass-Produced Fantasies for Women*. Hamden, Conn.: Archon, 1982.

Newlin, Margaret. "The Suicide Bandwagon." *Critical Quarterly* 14 (1972): 367-78.

Newman, Charles. *The Art of Sylvia Plath: A Symposium*. Bloomington: Indiana UP, 1970.

Oberg, Arthur. *Modern American Lyric: Lowell, Berryman, Creeley, and Plath*. New Brunswick: Rutgers UP, 1978.

————. "Sylvia Plath and the New Decadence." Butscher 177-85.

Ostriker, Alicia Suskin. *Writing like a Woman*. Ann Arbor: U of Michigan P, 1983.

————. *Stealing the Language: The Emergence of Women's Poetry in America*. Boston: Beacon P, 1986.

Paglia, Camille. *Sexual Personae: Art and Decadence from Nefertiti to Emily Dickenson*. New York: Vintage, 1991.

Pearson, Carol, and Katherine Pope. *The Female Hero in American and British Literature*. New York: R. R. Bowker, 1981.

Plath, Sylvia. *The Bell Jar*. 1963. Toronto: Bantam, 1981.

————. *The Collected Poems*. Ed. Ted Hughes. New York: Harper, 1981.

Poe, Edgar Allan. "The Philosophy of Composition." 1846. *Selections from the Critical Writings of Edgar Allen Poe*. 2nd ed. Ed. F. C. Prescott. New York: Gordian, 1981. 150-67.

Rich, Adrienne. "When We Dead Awaken: Writing as Re-Vision." 1971. *On Lies, Secrets, and Silence: Selected Prose 1966–78*. New York: Norton, 1979. 33-50.

Romano, John. "Sylvia Plath Reconsidered." *Commentary* 57 (April 1974): 47-52.

Rosenblatt, Jon. *Sylvia Plath: The Poetry of Initiation*. Chapel Hill: U of North Carolina P, 1979.

Rosowki, Susan J. "The Novel of Awakening." *Genre* 12.3 (Fall 1979): 313-39. Rpt. in Bloom *Kate Chopin* 43-60.

Schwartz, Murray M., and Christopher Bollas. "The Absence at the Center: Sylvia Plath and Suicide." *Criticism, a Quarterly for Literature and the Arts* 18.2 (Spring 1976): 147-72.

Showalter, Elaine. *The Female Malady: Women, Madness, and English Culture, 1830-1980*. New York: Pantheon, 1985.

Spangler, George M. "Neglected Fiction: Kate Chopin's *The Awakening*: A Partial Dissent." *Novel: A Forum on Fiction* 4 (1970): 249-55.

Smith, Stan. "Attitudes Counterfeiting Life: The Irony of Artifice in Sylvia Plath's *The Bell Jar*." *The Critical Quarterly* 17 (1975): 247-60. Rpt. in Bloom *Kate Chopin* 33-48.

Stevenson, Anne. *Bitter Fame: A Life of Sylvia Plath*. Boston: Houghton Mifflin, 1989.

Tennyson, Alfred Lord. "The Lady of Shallot." *The Poems of Tennyson*. Ed. Christopher Ricks. London: Longmans, 1969. 361.

Tolstoy, Leo. *Anna Karenina*. 1875-7. Trans. Leonard J. Kent and Nina Berberova. New York: Modern Library, 1965.

Tillet, Margaret. "On Reading *Madame Bovary*." *On Reading Flaubert*. London: Oxford, 1961. Rpt. in *Madame Bovary and the Critics: A Collection of Essays*. Ed. B. F. Bart. New York: New York UP, 1966. 1-25.

Van Dyne, Susan R. "Fueling the Phoenix Fire: Manuscripts of Sylvia Plath's 'Lady Lazarus'." *The Massachusetts Review* 24 (1983): 395-410. Rpt. in Bloom *Sylvia Plath* 133-48.

Veblen, Thorstein. *The Theory of the Leisure Class: An Economic Study in the Evolution of Institutions*. New York: Macmillan, 1899. Rpt. in Culley 138-40.

Wagner, Linda W., ed. *Critical Essays on Sylvia Plath*. Boston: G. K. Hall, 1984.

————. "Introduction." Wagner 1-24.

Wagner-Martin, Linda. *Sylvia Plath: A Biography*. New York: Simon, 1987.

Wharton, Edith. *The House of Mirth*. 1905. New York: Scribner's, 1933.

Wolff, Geoffrey. "*The Bell Jar*: A Review." 1971. Rpt. In *Sylvia Plath: The Critical Heritage*. Ed. Linda W. Wagner. London: Rutledge, 1988. 113.

Woolf, Virginia. *A Room of One's Own*. 1929. New York: Harcourt, 1957.

Ziff, Larzer. "*The American 1890s: Life and Times of a Lost Generation*." New York: Viking, 1966.

Zwerdling, Alex. *Virginia Woolf and the Real World*. Berkley: U of California P, 1986.